D1473072

Banker's Handbook for Strategic Planning

How To Develop and Implement A Successful Strategy

Douglas V. Austin

Mark S. Mandula

BANKERS PUBLISHING COMPANY

Bankers Management Series

Library of Congress Cataloging-in-Publication Data

Austin, Douglas V.
    Banker's handbook for strategic planning.

    (Bankers management series)
    Bibliography: p.
    Includes index.
    1. Bank management—United States.   2. Strategic
planning—United States.   3. Banks and banking—
United States.   I. Mandula, Mark S.   II. Title.
III. Series.
HG1615.A99   1985   332.1'2'068   85-9026
ISBN 0-87267-058-9

Executive Editor: Robert M. Roen
Managing Editor: Nancy Long Coleman
Cover design: Karen Mason

Contents

About the Authors

Douglas V. Austin is owner and president of Douglas Austin and Associates, a consulting company specializing in assisting banks in strategic planning and other management situations. He is also Professor of Finance at the University of Toledo.

Dr. Austin has taught banking and finance on the college level for the past 25 years. He also held the position of economist for the Federal Reserve Bank of Cleveland. He has been a speaker at various financial and banking meetings and has participated in over 200 presentations at national and regional levels. He has written three books on banking and over 170 articles on banking structure, competition, and performance.

Mark S. Mandula is vice president of Douglas Austin and Associates. He is the author of many articles on banking and of BANKWORTH, a software package designed to value commercial bank common stock on a microcomputer. He holds an M.B.A. from the University of Toledo.

Preface

Strategic planning is necessary and vital to the survival of banks. It is the orderly and logical planning of the future course of the bank, permitting participation by the board of directors, management, and bank employees. After years of financial consulting to the banking industry, we are extremely aware of the lack of strategic planning in banks, especially those less than $250 million in size. This book is intended to assist bankers in developing strategic plans that will direct the future course and financial performance of their banks, and in the long run, serve the community better.

This is a "how to" book. To assist in your understanding, we have deliberately attempted to provide procedures and timetables to aid the management and the board of directors in performing strategic planning. However, don't expect absolutely fantastic results the first year. The process itself becomes more sophisticated through practice in each ensuing year. Therefore, the second and third years will bring much more sophisticated results than the first year. We believe that by using the financial planning models and procedures within this book, you can run your bank more efficiently under a steady philosophical course of direction.

This work ties together, through detailed examples and descriptions, a practical explanation of strategic planning, and how you can do your job of strategic planning at your bank. Chapter 2 talks about the changing financial environment, and the role strategic planning plays in such an environment. Chapter 3 analyzes the steps in the strategic planning process and is coupled with chapter 4 which outlines the timetables for development of a strategic planning model. Chapter 5 outlines a series of data sources which will assist you in preparing your strategic plan. Chapters 6 and 7 outline long term planning, goals and objectives, and short term planning and budgeting. Chapters 8 and 9 switch gears and explain the role of the board of directors and the role of management in the development of strategic planning and the overall operation of the bank. Chapter 10 involves the microcomputer, and occasionally the mainframe, in the strategic planning process. In addition, chapter 10 analyzes the role of the microcomputer and its applications through "how to" examples. Without accountability and review the best laid plans can go astray; chapter 11 analyzes the accountability and review function not only as it is involved in strategic planning but also in other aspects of bank management. Chapter 12 outlines the interfacing of the strategic plan with the bank operations departments. Chapter 13 presents a review technique which is termed Situation Analysis.

We have taken into consideration the increasing importance of computers and have outlined their use in the planning process of banks. Most banks don't need to have large mainframes; almost any of the strategic planning techniques presented in this book can be done on a small microcomputer with adequate memory capacity. The biggest drawback, because microcomputer education in commercial banking is still relatively weak, may be to find someone within the commercial bank who can use the computer to assist in this strategic planning.

We believe that microcomputer analysis will increase the sophistication in the strategic planning process, both short and long term. It will be necessary for the management and the board of directors of banks to develop this expertise to assist in the achievement of the bank's objectives.

We are indebted to Craig D. Bernard, an MBA graduate of the University of Toledo, whose assistance was invaluable. Craig assisted in the preparation of the research material, edited the drafts, and worked on the whole manuscript. We greatly appreciate his contribution to the total effort.

We wish to recognize the College of Business Administration of the University of Toledo. We also acknowledge the contributions of our colleagues at the University of Toledo and the business community for assistance in the reworking and redrafting of this manuscript. Without their efforts, the book would not have been as cohesive as it is. Finally, we acknowledge the bank manager and/or director whose potential and current planning was strong motivation to write such a book.

1
Strategic Planning: The Key for Survival

This book is designed to make you a better strategic planner. Planning is necessary for survival. Without knowing where you are going, it is unlikely that you will get there. Strategic planning is the road map for survival. It focuses the attention of the bank's Board of Directors and the management and helps determine where they should be going and how to get there. It especially identifies where the pitfalls are over the short-term. Without planning, the operational and financial performance of the bank will be less than optimal and the overall objectives and goals of the institution may be difficult to achieve.

Strategic Planning Defined

The term "strategic planning" is a buzz word. We have been reading articles for the past several years on the advantages and disadvantages of calling the concept strategic planning. Some authors and speakers want to call it "strategic management" or simply "planning." Others don't believe in the concept at all. Regardless, the principal is still there—whatever we call it. Strategic planning is an organized thought process, participated in by employees, management, and the Board of Directors. The ultimate result is the determination of long-term goals and objectives of the corporation and the short-term implementation of *specific* goals using techniques/tactics which will permit the corporation to meet these long-term goals and objectives. The term strategic planning is used throughout this book to indicate that planning should be more than haphazard and subjective. Strategic planning could also be defined as logical, objective, and continuous. Thus, the purpose of this book is to assist you to plan for the future of your institution, and prepare your institution for whatever is necessary for its survival.

No matter the size of the institution, a sound strategic plan is essential for success. Managers and supervisors in most large banks would not be able to operate without clear and precise goals and objectives. Most small and medium-sized banks, with more centralized management, would also do well to develop and implement a strategic plan. It is not difficult or time consuming to develop and implement a strategic plan. It is not difficult or time consuming to develop and implement a good plan and the results are easily measurable.

The Importance of Strategic Planning

Strategic planning is important in the survival of the commercial bank. Lack of strategic planning indicates a lack of foresight, goals, and objectives of the management and the Board of Directors. It is the process of strategic planning, not necessarily the end results, that are crucial to the bank's future course or direction. In fact, survival may not even be the key. Perhaps the result of the strategic planning is to sell out, leave the industry, and pay off the shareholders. Even selling is an affirmative decision reached after prolonged and objective analysis. And that's certainly better than most community banks do today.

The end result of strategic planning is the full involvement of the management and the Board of Directors (as proxy for the shareholders) in determining the future course of the bank. By developing this consensus, and by determining the strengths and weaknesses of the commercial bank, the institution will be stronger and more able to cope with the problems it faces.

An extremely important aspect of strategic planning is the involvement of the outside directors in the planning process. Since most outside directors are not bankers, and typically are not familiar with the professional expertise necessary to run a bank on a day-to-day basis, their involvement in the planning process can increase their knowledge of the banking field. More importantly to the management of the bank, it can make them aware of the administrative and operational problems faced by bankers on a day-to-day basis. The expertise of the Board of Directors is quite different from that of the professional bankers. But, generally, the more the directors know the problems commercial bankers face, the better they will do their jobs as directors. Furthermore, good results from strategic planning will result in an improved degree of knowledge of the problems faced by the commercial bank.

The strategic planning process forces these day-to-day bankers to examine what will happen one, three, five, or ten years out in the future, and whether their livelihoods, occupations, and quiet lives will be protected through the successful operation of their employer. Commercial bankers gain perception of the overall impact of planning upon the operations of their institutions. Additionally, the commercial bankers often gain the insight that their forest encompasses all the trees and that the fires they face each day are not consuming, but simply brush fires in relation to the overall environment of the banking industry.

By the time you finish the book you should understand not only the overall parameters of strategic planning but how it impacts your bank. The use of practical examples throughout this book help to start the strategic planning process. The first year will not be perfect. However, utilizing the planning process the first year will assist you and your staff to become better planners the second year. The mistakes you make the first year will become evident as you go through the second year's planning process. Furthermore, keep in mind that as you make the mistakes, you can always change a decision. Strategic planning is a calculated business risk where you as management or members of the Board of Directors, attempt to determine where your commercial bank is going over the next five to ten years, and then attempt to implement specific policies and procedures to assist in the process. If you've guessed wrong, the FDIC can close your bank. Moreover, you will cause your family to go bankrupt and consequently destroy your reputation. On the other hand, what happens if you don't plan? Then your shareholders can sue you—they won't close the bank, but they can certainly ruin your reputation and make a dent in your wealth. Those financial institutions that do not aggressively change as the environment changes will be swept away in the flood waters of efficiency and competency, never to be heard from again.

Commercial bankers and members of the Board of Directors really have two choices. You can either take risks and plan as appropriately as you can, revising when necessary, or, you can simply sit back and not strategically plan at all. If the latter avenue is taken, there would be no grand plan where you would be six months or six years down the line, and many financial institutions have survived that way for the past fifty years. Unfortunately, these banks are not surviving that way today, and their lack of planning often places them in a position where they must sell, because of lack of management succession, bad loan portfolios, low earnings, or a series of major shareholders who want to get more liquid and sell their bank stock quickly. Any way you look at it, the importance of strategic planning might not stop this type of financial institution from selling, but it certainly would give them the voluntary ability to sell or not to sell based upon their appropriate operational philosophies and procedures.

"How To" Book

Strategic planning is a "how to" process. Thus, if you can't "do" learning "how to" is extremely important. We have included specific policies, procedures and examples to assist you in strategically planning your commercial bank. These are illustrative—not definitive. If there is anything we have learned in over twenty-five years of combined consulting experience it is that no two financial institutions are the same. The same general approaches can work for almost every financial institution—but each financial institution has its own personality, character, and way of doing things. Therefore, these policies, procedures, and specific examples should be used as guidelines and illustrations, not as axioms, because they can be modified to meet your own situation.

MicroComputerization

In this book we attempt to show you how strategic planning can be done on a microcomputer. Strategic planning is quantitative as well as qualitative, and the microcomputer permits you to develop alternative scenarios of the future with a great deal of clarity and definitiveness. Furthermore, it is impossible to do sophisticated strategic planning for the next five to ten years for your reorganization without a microcomputer or its equivalent. As you will see as you go through this book, the role of the computer is extremely important and should not be discounted. If you don't have a computer, get one. If you have one, but you don't know how to use it, get help.

Summary

Planning is essential for survival. Strategic planning is simply the orderly progression of planning to a logical objective or goal. Strategic planning for community banks is the key for their survival over the next ten to twenty years. Strategic planning is not the panacea for success. It may indicate that your bank is going to fail unless you make radical changes. Strategic planning should be used to determine the future course of your bank. Without it, the future will determine the course of your bank.

The remainder of this book will outline the necessary steps in the strategic planning process, a timetable for such a program, and sources of information available to you for purposes of strategic planning. In addition, the roles of the Board of Directors and management, both prior to and after the strategic planning process, will be analyzed. Finally, the interface between strategic planning and bank operations will be examined. This outline gives you an indication of exactly how strategic planning fits into the operation of your financial institution, and how you can improve the strategic planning process.

2

The Changing Financial Structure

The commercial banking industry has changed significantly in the last decade. Most states have liberally expanded their banking structural laws to allow the formation of multi-bank and one-bank holding companies, mergers, acquisitions, and consolidations of commercial bank and branches, and the rapid expansion of bank branching. These changes have also resulted in the increased ability of commercial banks to expand within their states and into other states to compete over much wider product and service areas. Additionally, commercial banking organizations such as Citicorp have been permitted to acquire ailing and floundering savings and loan associations, such as Fidelity Savings and Loan Association of Oakland, CA., First Federal Savings and Loan Association of Chicago, IL., and the New Biscayne Federal Savings and Loan Association of Miami, FL. Savings and loan associations have also been able to hop-scotch their way across the United States and expand more significantly than commercial banks in many political jurisdictions.

Prior to 1978, the most significant aspect of the commercial banking industry was its fixed rate, regulated, liability structure. Demand deposits were not permitted to pay interest, and all other depository sources, such as passbook savings, statement savings, and certificates of deposit had fixed ceiling rates. True, there were differentials between the maximum interest rate commercial banks could pay compared to savings and loan associations, mutual savings banks, credit unions, and other nonbanking financial intermediaries, but all the depository financial intermediaries had fixed ceiling rates regulated by supervisory authorities. The community banks, which depend upon non-deposit liability sources for any major degree of funding, knew their cost of funds pretty well at any one point in time. Profitable operations took place by pricing loans and investing funds at rates with enough net interest margin to be profitable. Most bankers simply looked at the bottom line at the end of the year, and if it was larger in terms of profits than the year before, it had been a good year. It was almost impossible to fail as a commercial bank without having someone deliberately embezzle bank funds through misapplication or misappropriation. This is not to say that there were no commercial bank failures prior to 1978. Commercial banks did fail in the short-term period prior to 1978, as is still true today, due to uncollectable commercial loans or fraud. In fact, in 1982 the First National Bank in Humboldt, Iowa failed due to the theft of the *entire* investment portfolio.

As stated, there was little risk and uncertainty in the commercial banking industry prior to 1978. All costs of funds were known, and fixed. Therefore, commercial banking was less risky and uncertain than it is today.

1978—The First Step

In July, 1978, President Carter signed legislation that created the money market certificate and the small savers certificate. The money market certificate, with a six month contractual maturity, a $10,000 minimum investment, and interest rates tied to the treasury bill rate, permitted interest rates considerably above the fixed 2-8 years certificate of deposit rates. The small saver certificates had a 2 1/2 year maturity, minimum deposits of $2,500 and a variable rate, set weekly, which was oriented to the treasury bond rate.

The introduction of these types of certificates opened the flood gate to higher costs of funding for community banks. This one step, which coupled increased risk and uncertainty in the commercial banking industry, has led to the importance of strategic planning. Let us illustrate the importance of these new savings/investment instruments. In March, 1978, the entire money market mutual fund industry had outstanding deposit totals of $5,000,000,000. By December 14, 1982, the money market mutual fund industry deposit totals had grown to $230,000,000,000. In contrast, it took the entire commercial banking industry 200 years to get to the $200,000,000,000 level.

Inflation

Almost as important as the growth of the money market instruments, inflationary conditions of the United States played a large role in increasing the risk and uncertainty involved in commercial banking. For example, the annualized inflation rate has moved from 11.3% in 1979 to 13.5% in 1980 and 10.4%, 6.1% and 3.2% in 1981, 1982, and 1983 respectively. By 1984 inflation had been brought under control with an annualized rate of 3.6% (we don't quite believe that every time you lose less purchasing power the inflationary trend is brought under control, but in comparison to previous years this has been the case). At the same time, interest rates finally came down in 1983. Between 1979 and 1983, the prime rate changed 87 times. The prime interest rate between January 1, 1979 and January 1, 1983 ranged from a low of 11% to a high of 21 1/2%. Unfortunately, for those lending and borrowing, the rates frequently went up and down, peaking several times before returning to lower levels. These were conditions of instability and uncertainty. Commercial banks faced with noncompetitive interest rate ceilings and financial instruments, such as the money market certificates, were unable to compete with the non-depository financial intermediaries. Commercial banks were not alone, however. The savings and loan associations, the mutual savings banks, and the credit unions, which had the majority of their deposit sources under fixed rate conditions, also suffered from the significant interest rate fluctuations.

Impact of DIDMCA

In March, 1980, Congress passed the Depository Institution Deregulation and Monetary Control Act (DIDMCA). We are not going to restate chapter and verse from DIDMCA, but we will review those features of the bill that have impacted the financial structure and environment of the commercial banking industry, since 1980.

1. A system was put in place to establish uniform reserve requirements for all commercial banks and other depository financial institutions. By 1988, all depository financial institutions with transaction accounts, regardless of their chartering status, must keep reserves at the Federal Reserve System. This will eliminate the entire issue of membership in the Federal Reserve System, and eliminate the differential between favorable state reserve requirements versus those of state chartered banks and national banks with Federal Reserve membership.

2. All depository financial institutions were permitted to offer negotiable orders of withdrawal (NOW), which are interest bearing checking accounts.

Prior to 1980, commercial banks had been the only depository financial institutions permitted to offer *non-interest* bearing checking accounts. But, due to DIDMCA and consumer confusion all depository financial institutions were permitted to offer NOW accounts. This made these other depository financial institutions more competitive than they were previously, with a full range of products and services.

3. In addition, new lending powers were permitted to non-bank depository financial institutions. Commercial banks had been the only depository financial institutions with commercial lending powers. DIDMCA permitted savings and loan associations and mutual savings banks to offer commercial loans. Furthermore, savings and loan associations and mutual savings banks, which previously had limited consumer installment powers, mostly enacted state by state, were permitted through DIDMCA to become nationwide powers in the consumer finance market. This new power resulted in direct competition with those financial institutions already established in the market—especially the commercial banks. These are important long-term competitive considerations.

4. The trust business had been limited to the commercial banking industry or trust companies. DIDMCA, through the implementation of trust powers, permitted savings and loan associations and mutual savings banks to establish trust departments. This was another example of an increasing competitive environment.

5. By far, the most important change was the elimination, through a phase-out period, of all interest rate ceilings on prime deposits at commercial banks, savings and loan associations, mutual savings banks, and credit unions. Soon all interest rate ceilings (with the exception of the ceiling on passbook savings) will have been eliminated. This means that, between 1980 and 1985, all of the intricate machinery that was set up to establish maximum interest rates ceilings on different types of savings and time deposits, will have been dismantled with the exception of passbook savings. However, these ceilings are to be phased out in 1986. Credit unions have eliminated all savings and time deposit ceilings.

The removal of interest rate ceilings was significant, not only because it increased competition between the commercial bank and other depository financial institutions, but also because DIDMCA resulted in the increased average cost of funds in the commercial banking industry. Although it is a gross generalization to note the following, the median cost of funds (excluding demand deposits) in 1979 for the commercial banking industry was 6.72%. By 1982, this annualized figure had risen to 10.38%. This means that generally the cost of funds at commercial banks, as well as at other depository financial institutions, went through the roof, and changed the entire environment of the industry.

Commercial banks woke up after the passage of DIDMCA and found themselves in a less favorable competitive position. Yet, they had not been given the tools necessary to compete against the money market mutual funds. In 1980, 1981, and 1982 the commercial banking industry growth was significantly impeded by the money market funds success, and the inflationary impact noted earlier. Needless to say, the same was true for the other depository financial intermediaries. Under tremendous pressure, changes were made in 1982 which have had a profound affect upon the changing financial structure and environment faced by community banks.

Garn-St. Germain Depository Institutions Act

The Garn-St. Germain Depository Institutions Act of 1982 (DIA) is as important to the operation of commercial banks as the 1980 act. The Garn-St. Germain Act continued to materially change the ability of commercial banks to operate under these conditions. The specific aspects of the Garn-St. Germain which are important for our discussion are the following:

1. The money market deposit account was created. This non-minimum balance, daily interest deposit account is able to compete directly against money market mutual funds. Depository financial institutions, including banks, savings and loans, mutual savings banks, and credit unions can offer such a financial instrument at any minimum they desire, change the interest over periods of time, and compete directly with the money market mutual funds. A depository financial institution may even have a competitive advantage. The daily interest, from date of deposit to date of withdrawal, may result in an overall greater return to the investor than the money market mutual fund. This instrument has had a tremendous impact upon the ability of the commercial banks to survive and compete since 1982. In December 1982, money market deposits reached a level of $43,200,000,000. This increased drastically during 1983 to $372.4 billion dollars. The money market mutual fund industry will continue to compete, but its growth trend has greatly slowed or even reversed.

2. Garn-St. Germain created a priority system for permitting interstate and cross-industry acquisition of failing and floundering depository financial institutions. The priority system is relatively simple, although its implementation since 1982 has been anything but simple. If a depository financial institu-

tion is considered to be failing or floundering by the appropriate supervisory agencies, then bidding to acquire the institution can take place on the following basis: 1) same type of depository financial institution within the same state; 2) same type of depository financial institution from other states; 3) a different type of depository financial institution within the same state; 4) a different type of depository financial institution from out of state.

This has permitted Citicorp to acquire savings and loan associations in California, Florida, and Illinois. It has permitted savings and loan associations headquartered in California to acquire savings and loan associations in Texas, Missouri, Illinois, and Florida. It has permitted savings and loan associations or mutual savings banks in New York to acquire failing or floundering institutions within their state or outside. This aspect of the Garn-St. Germain Bill (DIA) is designed to contravene state law and to permit interstate acquisitions (contrary to the Douglas Amendment to the Bank Holding Company Act of 1956, or the McFadden Act) when it is considered to be in the public interest that such depository financial institutions should be acquired to insure their continuity rather than their liquidation. This aspect of the act has been used in over thirty cases since 1982, and will continue to be used as long as state law impedes the acquisition of financial institutions by other financial institutions within the same state. Several states, such as Illinois and Washington, have passed emergency legislation permitting major financial institutions to be "saved" through the utilization of the DIA. As the decade continues, the increased passage of state legislation may make this aspect of the Garn-St. Germain bill less applicable but it has been an important feature, and has brought competitive entry into many local markets. For example, Ft. Wayne, Indiana, is a regional center in Northeastern Indiana, and within that marketplace there were six commercial banks and four savings and loans operating as of June, 1983. In one fell swoop, three savings and loan associations which were failing and floundering, were acquired by the Standard Federal Savings and Loan Association of Troy, Michigan. This changed the entire competitive environment within Ft. Wayne, Indiana, because of the introduction of Standard Federal. Additionally, this combination resulted in the merger of two of the major commercial banks within Ft. Wayne in order to compete in the changed financial environment. This is just one example. Most of you will know of others that have taken place within your state, if not within your community. These combinations will continue, and, from a public policy standpoint, it certainly is better for this type of acquisition to take place than to have bank runs and liquidations. However, the changing competitive environment changes the way community bankers must operate.

3. Garn-St. Germain also created the Super NOW account. This NOW

account has a $2500 minimum balance, with interest that can be paid at a level higher than the fixed interest rate of 5 1/4% for commercial banks and 5 1/2% for thrift institutions. The Super NOW account has been primarily stagnant since 1982, but DIA permitted its creation.

What Have All the Changes Meant?

In essence, DIDMCA and Garn-St. Germain created an entirely new competitive environment. The commercial banking industry no longer consists only of primary depository financial institutions. Other depository financial institutions were given essentially equal depository and lending powers. Increased competition has taken place in the market through the growth and development of non-depository financial intermediaries, and DIDMCA and DIA permitted expanded interest rate competition on the liability side. In addition, the DIA permitted the saving of floundering and failing institutions through interstate and intrastate acquisitions by like or unlike depository financial institutions. All these new powers cut deeply into the favorable position of the commercial banking industry.

The Effect Upon Profitability

Many banks have suffered from the changing environment. However, not all commercial banks or other depository financial institutions have been affected negatively. Those financial institutions able to react quickly through appropriate management have suffered the least. What DIDMCA and DIA did was to significantly increase the cost of funds but not materially change the asset rate of returns for community banks. Those commercial banks and other depository financial institutions that were able to quickly change their asset portfolios to match their increasing cost of funds, have been those institutions that have managed the best over the past five years. Keep in mind that all of your depository rates on savings and time deposits have been floating freely, except for passbook savings accounts, since 1980 or 1982. On the other hand, the asset powers have not increased significantly. It has only been through the introduction of favorable rates that financial institutions could attempt to match income to the cost of funds in order to keep the appropriate net interest margin.

Needless to say, you can now go out of business through operational inefficiency. You don't have to wait for someone to steal the bank in order to go broke. You as bankers now have the opportunity to be managerially incompetent. This book will make sure that you strategically plan and understand the circumstances, so that in an increasingly risky and uncertain

environment—coupled with fluctuating asset and liability returns and costs—
you can manage to make a profit, and return to your investors appropriate
rates of return so that they will continue to support your efforts as a financial
institution. That has not been easy, and it won't get any easier, but this book
will assist you in solving some of the problems.

Interstate Banking, Reciprocity, Non-bank Banks, and the Overall Impact on Financial Structure and Environment

The impact of interstate banking reciprocity acts and the introduction of the
non-bank banks is resulting in even more competition. In the United States,
interstate banking has been limited by state law. For all intents and purposes,
interstate banking has not been permitted. West of the Mississippi River, there
has been some interstate banking due to distance and due to the more favorable state laws involved. Furthermore, most of this interstate banking was
permitted prior to the Bank Holding Company Act of 1956 as amended, and
was therefore in place prior to the institution of the Douglas Amendment to
the Bank Holding Company Act which prohibits, unless permitted by state
law, interstate ownership of bank holding company corporations (affiliates)
across state lines.

Interstate Banking
New York, Maine, and Alaska, are the only three states that permit full interstate banking. In the latter months of 1984, Key Bank, a $6,000,000,000 bank
holding company headquartered in Albany, New York had received approval
to acquire a Maine bank holding company and *Alaska Pacific Bancshares* an
Alaska Bank Holding Company. Interstate banking is not fully permitted
throughout the United States. On the other hand, as Figure 2-1 indicates, there
are a great number of interstate banking operations in the United States. A
study by David Whitehead indicates that, as of January 1, 1983 there were
7,840 interstate offices of out-of-state banking organizations. This number was
noted as conservative and it is our opinion that by early 1985, this number will
have risen to over 10,000 offices.

Reciprocity
As a means of getting around the Douglas Amendment's prohibition against
interstate banking, several states have entered into their own interstate regional compacts, known familiarly as reciprocity. These interstate regional

Figure 2-1   Summary of Interstate Activity

| | Grandfathered | | | | | |
| | Domestic | | | Foreign A | | |
Location	Holding* Companies	Banks	Branches	Holding* Companies	Banks	Branches
Alabama						
Alaska						
Arizona	1	1	171			
Arkansas						
California				8	8	135
Colorado	1	3	5			
Connecticut						
Delaware						
District of Columbia						
Florida	2	22	141			
Georgia						
Hawaii				1	1	15
Idaho	2	2	103			
Illinois	1	6	5	1	1	0
Indiana						
Iowa	1	11	32			
Kansas						
Kentucky						
Louisiana						
Maine						
Maryland	1	2	28			
Massachusetts						
Michigan						
Minnesota						
Mississippi						
Missouri						
Montana	3	25	18			
Nebraska	1	5	11			
Nevada	1	1	72			
New Hampshire						
New Jersey						
New Mexico	1	5	29			
New York	1	1	8	3	3	32
North Carolina						
North Dakota	3	32	40			
Ohio						
Oklahoma						
Oregon	1	1	164			
Pennsylvania						
Puerto Rico				2	2	32
Rhode Island						
South Carolina						
South Dakota	2	6	72			
Tennessee	2	2	24			
Texas						
Utah	1	1	38			9
Vermont						
Virginia	1	2	78			
Washington	1	1	91			
West Virginia						
Wisconsin	3	6	7			
Wyoming	2	4	0			
TOTALS		139	1137		15	214

* The columns are not included in total number of offices per state.
U—Allow unrestricted entry.
F—Allow out-of-state acquisition of a failing bank.
R—Reciprocal agreements.
X—Allow entry of limited purpose banks.

| Foreign Banks | | | Limited Purpose Banks° | States With Interstate Banking Provisions° | Inter-state S&Ls° | Offices of 4(c)8 Subs | Loan Production Offices | Edge Act Corpor-ations | Total Offices Per State |
Agency	Edge	Branch							
					1	107	1		108
				U		4	1		5
						159			331
						3			3
63	2	2			2	521	22	23	776
					1	158	14		180
				R		64	1		65
			11	X		27	3	5	35
		1			2	2	3		6
22	6			R	7	372	6	25	594
10				R	2	253	8	5	276
2					2	39			57
					2	47			152
	3	36		#F	1	132	21	11	215
						99	1		100
				#		42	2		87
					1	78			78
				R	1	61			61
1						164	4	1	170
				U		1			1
				X	3	82	7		119
		4		R	1	68	6	3	81
						56	2		58
						34	5	4	43
						89			89
					1	75	6	2	83
					2	28	1		72
				X#		28	2		46
				X	1	21			94
						20	1		21
						110	2		112
						44			78
18	2	37		R	5	156	16	31	304
				R		367	3		370
						23	1		96
						310	8	4	322
						76	3		79
		7		M	4	83	7	3	265
		6				320	7	2	335
									34
				R		13			13
				R		229			229
			1	X		16			94
						159	14		199
					6	289	19	17	334
				RF	1	37	1		77
						4			4
			1	X	2	227	1		308
		10		F	2	114	3	6	225
						40			40
						39		1	53
					1	10			14
116	22	103	13	22	51	5500	202	143	7591

#—Allow expansion of grandfathered banks.
M—Allow acquisition of mutual savings banks.
A—Six of the foreign bank holding companies own only one U.S. bank, but the bank is located outside the home state of the foreign banking organization.
Source: Federal Reserve Bank of Atlanta. *Economic Review* 70.3 (March 1985): 18–19

compacts are designed to permit interstate competition between commercial banking organizations and other depository financial institutions. At the same time, these compacts often have the feature of excluding one or more states from their reciprocity. Nobody wants New York state in their compact group. In fact, in 1983, the New England states of Rhode Island, Massachusetts, and Connecticut entered into an interstate regional compact. This compact proposed affiliations to the Comptroller of the Currency and the Federal Reserve System. Approval was received, but it is being litigated by Citicorp, which did not like it that New York was excluded from the New England Compact. In the Southeast, several states have passed reciprocity laws permitting entry between banks of the several states. Furthermore, in the mid-west, some states have the opportunity of being in two or three reciprocity pacts. The purpose of these pacts is to permit regional interstate banking, while still keeping the wolf from your door. Ten years ago, the community bankers worried about the big banks from Detroit, Cleveland, Indianapolis, Chicago, or another big city bank entering their local markets. Today, the paranoia is still there. It just comes from a different location. For example, if your bank is located in Ohio, you may worry about the entry of Citicorp, Chase Manhattan, and Bank of America. You might be willing to keep away from those big guys by aligning yourself with another bank, so that in Ohio you will be competing only against Mellon National Corp, the big banks from Louisville, Indianapolis, and Detroit or other regional banks. In some ways, the entire idea of reciprocity is not whether you get shot by the firing squad, but simply what caliber of bullet they use when they shoot you. The issue of interstate banking and who will compete within your geographic market, has gone from an intrastate to an interstate question.

Should Citicorp or any other petitioner prevail, interstate regional compacts would not be as popular to the states, and the proliferation of regional reciprocity compacts would come to an end. On the other hand, if such regional compacts are held to be constitutional by the Supreme Court, then certain states could be excluded from regional compacts. Thus, the trend for interstate banking may be decided by the results of the Citicorp litigation against the New England Compact.

Non-Bank Banks

Since 1980, a new competitive depository financial institution has started to surface across the United States. It is the non-bank bank. The non-bank bank has risen because of a loophole in the definition of a bank in the Bank Holding Company Act of 1956 as amended. The Bank Holding Company Act defines a bank as a financial institution which accepts demand deposits *and* makes commercial loans. Thus, if a bank were to either not accept demand deposits, or not make commercial loans, it wouldn't be a bank, and therefore would lie outside the jurisdiction. The entire non-bank bank idea came about in 1980 with the attempt by Wilsher Oil to keep its New Jersey Bank. Unfortunately, Wilsher Oil attempted to make its bank a non-bank by simply giving notice to demand deposit customers that there was a fourteen day right of withdrawal, such as on savings accounts. The Supreme Court determined this was insufficient proof and rejected the Wilsher Oil attempts. However, corporate banking lawyers noted that if you either did not make big commercial loans or accept demand deposits you were outside the definition.

By December 1984, there were over 340 applications to the Comptroller of the Currency for non-bank banks. Almost all of these non-bank banks' applications have been made by the largest depository financial institutions, and most are centered in the rapidly growing economic development states such as Texas, California, Florida, North and South Carolina, Georgia, and the Southwestern states of Arizona and New Mexico. Other banks to submit non-bank bank applications are outside or within the major metropolitan centers such as Chicago, New York, and Washington, D.C. The Comptroller of the Currency waited until October, 1984 for Congress to pass legislation to prohibit the approval of these applications. However, Congress adjourned at the end of 1984 and did not reach a decision on the non-bank bank loophole. Thus, starting in October 1984 the Comptroller of the Currency started approving the non-bank bank applications. By December 1, 1984, over 77 had been approved, although none were doing business due to the lack of approval by the Federal Reserve. By January 1, 1985, approval by the Federal Reserve was still pending, and there is a question whether these applications will ever be approved. However, the entire idea of the non-bank bank is a way to cross state lines and circumvent the Douglas Amendment of the Bank Holding Company Act of 1956.

It should be noted that almost all of the non-bank applications chose not to make commercial loans. This would seem illogical, since commercial banks are supposed to make commercial loans. However, since most of the applications for non-bank banks have been made by national banks, and since national banks can operate loan production offices nationwide, it would be very logical for them to charter a non-bank bank which did not make commercial loans. These banks would then form a Loan Production Officer (LPO) in the same building and make commercial loans. This attempt to liberalize the interstate nature of commercial banking is another indication of the new and changing financial structure and the environment faced by community bankers. Needless to say, most community banks will not be fazed by interstate banking or from the competition of non-bank banks. But in some markets, including suburban markets of major metropolitan cities, there will be increased competition.

Financial Service Corporations

In addition to the proliferation of commercial banking organizations across state lines and the introduction of non-bank banks, financial service corporations increasingly become a competitive factor in many local banking markets. Financial service corporations are those organizations that have financially oriented services, and compete directly or indirectly with banks for the banking business. Figure 2-2 lists the major financial service corporations. The most important ones for local market competition today are Merrill Lynch, Pearce, Fenner & Smith; Sears Roebuck & Company; Prudential Bache & Co.; and American Express. In fact, all of these own their own bank or non-banks in addition to competing in allied fields. Sears Roebuck, for example, has a commercial bank, a savings and loan grouping in California, a major residential real estate brokerage firm (Caldwell Banker), the brokerage firm of Dean Witter, Reynolds, as well as the All State Insurance subsidiary. Prudential Bache is an insurance company and a national investment banking firm. American Express has the Shearson American Express subsidiary which is also a national brokerage firm. Furthermore, these institutions have cash management accounts, travel agencies, travelers checks, money orders, and make certain types of loans in direct competition with large and small banks alike. Sears Roebuck has established financial centers in many of its major stores, and some of these are located in local markets in direct competition with community banks.

In essence, non-banking corporations are attempting to get into the banking field, while commercial banking organizations are attempting to get into the allied fields. The Glass-Steagall Act is under siege, not only from commercial banks trying to get back into investment banking after fifty years, but from investment bankers trying to hold the banker back. At the same time, non-bank bank proliferation, the establishment of banks by financial service corporations, and money market mutual funds, are attempts by the non-banking intermediaries to get into the banking business.

There is no way to determine what is going to happen in this area over the next several years. But this battle will continue to heat up until Congress

Figure 2-2   Financial Services Corporations ($ Millions)

	By: Equity		By: Net Income		By: Assets	
Rank	Name	($)	Name	($)	Name	($)
1	State Farm	4,621	Bank America	645	Citicorp	114,920
2	Bank America	3,908	State Farm	564	Bank America	111,617
3	Citicorp	3,891	Aetna Life	562	Chase	76,190
4	Allstate	3,764	Citicorp	507	Prud. Bache	62,744
5	Aetna Life	3,281	Metropol. Life	479	Man. Hanover	55,522
6	Prud. Bache	2,952	Amex/Shearson	432	J. P. Morgan	51,991
7	GMAC	2,752	Allstate	397	Metropol. Life	48,310
8	Chase	2,688	J. P. Morgan	368	Continental	42,089
9	Travelers	2,643	Travelers	366	Chemical	41,342
10	Amex/Shearson	2,306	Chase	365	Aetna	36,753
11	Conn. General	2,234	Conn. General	317	Equitable Life	N/A
12	Contin. (N.Y.)	2,123	Prud. Bache	299	Bankers Trust	34,202
13	Metropol. Life	2,055	AIG	288	GMAC	33,047
14	J. P. Morgan	2,018	INA	279	First Inter.	32,110
15	INA	1,842	TransAmerica	245	First Chicago	28,699
16	Man. Hanover	1,709	US Fid. & Gar.	241	Security Pac.	27,790
17	AIG	1,592	First Inter.	233	Wells Fargo	23,638
18	Ford Credit	1,537	GMAC	231	Amex/Shearson	21,977
19	Continential	1,525	Man. Hanover	230	Travelers	21,638
20	TransAmerica	1,485	Continential	244	Allstate	20,845

Source: "Bankings' New Peer Group," L. A. Frieder, *The Bankers Magazine*, 166: 76–82. September/October 1983

enacts reform and/or drafts legislation. There seems to be a return to a greater degree of free competition. And, except for the massive number of bank failures which are cause for reregulation rather than continued deregulation, there will be a proliferation of the financial service corporations and increased competition in local markets.

Bankers should be concerned about these financial service corporations. Money market mutual funds' toll free numbers; cash management accounts that compete with bank services, some types of loans made through the mail or through credit card extensions, result in increased competition. On the other hand, commercial bankers, knowing that they are facing a larger degree of competition, can provide faster, more convenient, and more personal service. Increased competition does not mean that the bank will flounder and fail. In fact, it may do just the opposite. It will be up to you as bankers to strategically plan your future by understanding the degree and types of competition within your market and therefore be able to competitively circumvent the competition from other financial service corporations.

Bank Holding Companies

The bank holding company movement continues to be pervasive and significant within the banking industry. As Figure 2-3 indicates, multi-bank holding companies have continued to expand during the 70s and early 1980s. Only three states (Indiana, Mississippi and Kansas) do not permit the multi-bank holding company structural form, and Indiana and Kansas have legislation pending to permit the multi-bank holding company form of organization.

Multi-bank holding companies now control approximately 80% of all of the assets in the commercial banking industry. This trend is significantly upward since 1956, the year of the Bank Holding Company Act. At the same time, the number of affiliates within bank holding companies has declined. This trend is primarily due to the consolidation statutes available in many states, which permit the bank holding company organizations to operate as a state-wide branching system, or regional branching systems, rather than as a straight holding company affiliate organization.

The most significant phenomenon over the past decade has been the rise of the one-bank holding company structural form. In 1971, there were only 112 bank holding companies throughout the United States. On January 1, 1984, there were 5371 bank holding companies in the United States. More than one per day has been chartered during 1984. In the following paragraphs we will examine the advantages and disadvantages of the one-bank holding company. From such examination, the importance of the one-bank holding company to the survival of the community bank will become evident. Thus, one aspect of strategic planning for community banks is to establish the type of organizational structure that will provide the most advantages, and the least disadvantages, in terms of survival as a commercial banking organization over the next two decades. We recommend that the one-bank holding company structure be chosen in order to assist in the perpetuity of the organization.

Advantages of a One-Bank Holding Company

The formation of a one-bank holding company is simply the legal reorganization of the commercial bank into a corporate form in which the holding company controls the outstanding stock of the commercial bank. There are

Figure 2-3   Bank Holding Companies in the United States

State	12/31/82	12/31/83	Change
Alabama	38	59	21
Alaska	5	5	0
Arizona	10	13	3
Arkansas	67	97	30
California	120	172	52
Colorado	145	162	17
Connecticut	10	10	0
Delaware	13	21	8
District of Columbia	15	17	2
Florida	105	139	34
Georgia	90	116	26
Hawaii	5	5	0
Idaho	11	12	1
Illinois	426	489	63
Indiana	107	141	34
Iowa	308	330	22
Kansas	385	417	32
Kentucky	73	120	47
Louisiana	85	125	40
Maine	6	7	1
Maryland	21	21	0
Massachusetts	28	29	1
Michigan	47	53	6
Minnesota	330	359	29
Mississippi	46	60	14
Missouri	220	252	32
Montana	54	60	6
Nebraska	291	312	21
Nevada	3	3	0
New Hampshire	8	10	2
New Jersey	26	30	4
New Mexico	30	33	3
New York	80	85	5
North Carolina	12	19	7
North Dakota	75	83	8
Ohio	35	39	4
Oklahoma	301	332	31
Oregon	14	18	4
Pennsylvania	57	81	24
Puerto Rico	5	5	0
Rhode Island	11	11	0
South Carolina	5	13	8

Figure 2-3   (*continued*)

State	12/31/82	12/31/83	Change
South Dakota	52	62	10
Tennessee	83	119	36
Texas	426	500	74
Utah	24	25	1
Vermont	7	11	4
Virginia	16	23	7
Washington	17	21	4
West Virginia	12	30	18
Wisconsin	141	170	29
Wyoming	45	45	0
TOTAL	4546	5371	825

Source: Rand McNally International Bankers Directory, U.S. Master Edition 1983 & 1984

specific advantages that would accrue to the institution upon formation of a one-bank holding company.

The initial advantage is in the coporate tax area. When the parent company (the bank holding company) owns or controls over 80% of the stock of a subsidiary bank, it may elect, under Section 1501 of the Internal Revenue Code, to consolidate its corporate income tax returns. In addition, if the holding company owns 80% or more of the stock of the bank, intercorporate dividends paid by the bank to the holding company are not taxed. The interest expense incurred by the holding company for borrowed funds, which have been used to purchase bank stock, may then be deducted from the income of the bank. The important benefit is that the holding company financial statements reflect tax savings income from the bank in addition to the profit of the bank.

The second advantage of the one-bank holding company to the institution would be the ability to attract additional capital. The one-bank holding company allows for increased flexibility in the area of capital infusion. In recent years, many banks, particularly small to medium-size banks, have needed additional capital. Numerous commercial banks have either experienced a rapid increase in assets (greater than retained earnings) or have suffered significant losses which have cut into their capital position. Generally speaking, however, many banks cannot raise additional capital in the equity market because outstanding stock is currently selling well below book value. Thus, the sale of additional stock at market prices would greatly dilute present share-holders' equity.

On the other hand, these same banks find that they cannot borrow additional capital in the form of subordinated debt. If they did, they would exceed permissible regulatory guidelines for such borrowing. In recent years, the regulatory authorities have become dissatisfied with the use of subordinated debentures, formerly known as capital notes debentures. Due to this situation, the push today is for equity capital. The one-bank holding company permits the utilization of debt at the holding company level, which is then down-streamed to the subsidiary commercial bank. This technique is accepted as infusions of equity capital by the regulatory authorities. At the same time, due to the upstreaming of non-taxable dividends by the commercial bank holding company parent, the expenses incurred can be paid by the holding company.

The ability of a bank holding company to borrow through correspondent banks, institutional investors, and from the market directly, is greatly enhanced in the one-bank holding company structure. All parties are satisfied. The bank receives the additional capital it needs. And the supervisory agencies witness the infusion of additional equity capital into the bank.

The third benefit which would accrue to the institution under the one-bank holding company structure would be the increased ability to redeem stock. Without the holding company structure, repurchase of stock may drain funds from the bank which in turn would weaken the security of the depositors' funds. Conversely, bank holding companies are allowed to redeem up to 10% of their own stock without prior approval from the Federal Reserve Bank. If there is an opportunity to redeem more than 10% of the stock, permission must be received from the Federal Reserve Bank responsible for supervision of the holding company. This additional ability to redeem stock would accrue several very important benefits to the institution.

1. The ability to redeem stock gives greater responsibility and liquidity to the buyers of holding company stock. This helps create a strong secondary market for the holding company stock.
2. The increased redemption ability makes the stock more attractive to individual and corporate investors. The increased attractiveness may also increase the price of stock. This could occur when the supply of stock currently out in the financial community is reduced in relation to the demand for the stock.
3. The increased ability of the holding company to redeem its stock ef-

fectively permits the holding company to maintain a market in its stock. By maintaining a market in the holding company stock, the supply can be kept low and the price is therefore kept up.

An additional advantage of the one-bank holding company structure is that the bank could begin to diversify into other services. Federal Reserve Board regulations permit some diversification into various services by one-bank and other holding companies.

State and national commercial banks are limited in the types of subsidiaries that they may have attached to their banks. Over the past decade, the Federal Reserve System has expanded nonbanking activities for holding companies. Therefore, if the organization becomes a one-bank holding company, it may be prudent to begin to engage in nonbanking activities which the individual commercial bank may not be able to offer.

There are numerous reasons why a bank holding company should expand into nonbanking activities. Bank holding companies expand into nonbanking activities because they have limited opportunities to expand in their banking operations and/or they anticipate substantial benefits from expanding into nonbank activities. Bank holding companies receive benefits by expanding into nonbanking areas.

1. There are potentially higher returns by expanding into functional areas that provide higher returns than traditional banking. (For example, factoring and leasing.)
2. There may also be a potential risk reduction by diversifying among banking and nonbanking activities since returns are not equally sensitive to economic events of the local area.
3. An additional consideration is that risk may be reduced by controlling various affiliates. Financial problems of one affiliate may not necessarily jeopardize the financial status of the parent holding company. This allows one subsidiary of the bank to perform poorly in any one given year without affecting the overall performance of the entire organization.
4. An additional benefit of diversifying into nonbanking activities is that investors often view this as a positive development. Therefore, potentially higher market valuation could be achieved by investors who believe, other factors being equal, that a diversified bank holding company would achieve higher returns and/or lower risk than would a bank holding company that limits itself to traditional banking activities.

5. A final advantage of diversification is that the bank holding company has an opportunity to provide customers with a greater range of services, possibly at lower cost. As competition in the entire financial institution and investment area increases, it will be important for all commercial banks to begin to offer a smorgasbord of services or lose customers to other organizations.

Disadvantages of a One-Bank Holding Company

It would be myopic to ignore the negative aspects of a one-bank holding company. The following paragraphs briefly discuss the disadvantages.

A major disadvantage of the formation of any one-bank holding company is the danger in forming it without a legitimate, long-term purpose. Time and time again, since imitation is the most sincere form of flattery, commercial banks have reorganized into one-bank holding companies simply because their competitors and neighbors have. A commercial bank should not form a one-bank holding company unless there are legitimate business purposes for doing so. If a one-bank holding company is formed, and the management thereafter does not attempt to redeem stock, maintain the market price, purchase any other commercial banks, introduce nonbanking activities, or in any way use the new structural formation to their advantage, then the cost of formation is money down the drain.

There are costs in becoming and remaining a bank holding company. It costs anywhere from $20,000 to $60,000 to form a one-bank holding company. It costs approximately $10,000 a year, directly and indirectly, to remain a one-bank holding company. The costs should be compared to the benefits which would accrue to the commercial bank. If there is a legitimate business purpose for forming a one-bank holding company, such as the additional ability to attract capital, one has to compare these benefits to the costs involved in the formation of the one-bank holding company. Obviously, if the costs exceed the benefits, it would be imprudent for the management to move forward and form a one-bank holding company. On the other hand, in almost all situations, the benefits exceed the costs in relation to forming a one-bank holding company, and therefore it is most prudent for management to form a one-bank holding company.

A final disadvantage in the formation of a one-bank holding company is the time involved. Commercial banking is a regulated industry. A holding company cannot be set up overnight. Certain amounts of staff and management time will be needed to gather necessary information. Additionally, as previously mentioned, certain regulatory guidelines must be followed in a step-by-step fashion to complete the formation. The overall time frame, from the gathering of information to consummation, ranges from six months to up-ward of 1 1/2 to 2 years.

The Changing Face of Competition

Community banks are in the eye of a hurricane. Ten years ago, commercial banks competed only with other commercial banks, or so it was perceived. Today, commercial banks, whether they are community banks or major branch/holding companies systems, compete not only with commercial banks, but also with savings and loan associations, mutual savings banks, credit unions, government lending agencies, financial service corporations, money market mutual funds, and consumer and sales finance companies. Competition takes place not only locally, but also nationwide through 800 numbers, direct mail solicitations, mass media advertising, and other forms which directly affect the ability of the commercial bank to succeed. The commercial banker today should understand fully that competition comes from many directions, and not just from other commercial banks within the local community. Additionally, competition will continue to become even more intense in the years to come. Thus bankers must position themselves and their banks, through effective strategic planning, to meet all competitive efforts within the local community.

Anti-Trust Changes in Recent Years

Mergers and acquisitions have always played an important role in either the survival or expansion of commercial banks. Prior to DIDMCA and DIA, anti-trust rules were relatively straight-forward, and bankers pretty well knew whether they could merge or not merge under these rules. Commercial banks were considered to be competitive only with other commercial banks. Actual competition took place when banks were in actual and direct competition. Furthermore, prior to DIDMCA and Garn-St. Germain potential competition was not considered as a valuable doctrine in commercial banking anti-trust law.

The evolution of the depository industry and the changing face of competition has significantly altered the anti-trust aspects of mergers and acquisitions. DIDMCA and Garn-St. Germain have liberalized the competitive aspects in determining whether commercial bank mergers and/or acquisitions are anti-competitive.

There are two basic doctrines that apply to the competitive posture of any merger or acquisition; the relevant line of commerce also known as the relevant product line, and the relevant geographic section of the country also known as the relevant banking market. Anti-competitiveness therefore, is in essence a measure of the relevant product line and the relevant banking market. Providing anti-competitiveness is not a factor in a merger/acquisition transaction, most mergers/acquisitions will be approved unless there are negative factors concerning earnings, management, or capital adequacy.

The concepts of the relevant line of commerce and the relevant banking market have changed significantly in the past five years. For example, the relevant line of commerce from 1961 to 1975, and through all of the anti-trust litigation, was considered to be commercial banking. During this time, commercial banks were the only financial institutions to have demand deposits. The Supreme Court of the United States in its pronouncements indicated that commercial banks only competed with other commercial banks. However, this is no longer the case. The relevant line of commerce has been expanded, on a case by case basis, to include those depository financial institutions and non-bank financial intermediaries that compete directly and immediately with commercial banks within any given banking market. Thus, it is now permitted to include all types of competitors if it can be proven that these competitors are actually competing within the marketplace. At one extreme, all other non-bank competitors could be weighted equally with the commercial banks involved. At the least, competitors could be weighted based upon their impact within the marketplace. It is the burden of the merger/acquisition applicants to develop the information necessary for approval.

The relative geographic section of the country has not experienced radical change since enacting DIDMCA in 1980. However, given the same market size, increased competitors permit for an increased number of mergers and acquisitions without hitting anti-competitive thresholds. This can be seen in that almost every bank merger/acquisition has been approved since 1981, although there have been several reconsiderations due to insufficient data. Several studies by the Federal Reserve System in the past several years have indicated that mergers and acquisitions approved in recent years would not have been approved prior to DIDMCA and Garn-St. Germain.

As to the future definition of the relevant banking market, changes are expected. As intrastate banking becomes complete, and interstate banking barriers are broken down, the relevant banking market will increase in terms of geographical size. Thus, as the geographical boundaries of the relevant banking markets are enlarged the numbers of mergers and acquisitions will also increase. Bankers should plan for additional areas of geographic expansion as the restricted geographical barriers to banking evaporate. You, as the bankers of tomorrow, should consider almost any market available for entry. And, in a reciprocal fashion, you could assume that your relatively isolated stable banking market will be open to other entrants.

4-C8 Activities

Most community banks do not have nonbanking activities. Commercial banking organizations which have reorganized into multi-banks or one-bank holding companies are permitted to have certain nonbanking activities carried on through subsidiary corporations (4-C8 activities). The 4-C8 comes from Section 4 of Regulation Y of the Federal Reserve Act. Figure 2-4 indicates all of the 4-C8 permissible activities as of year end 1984. For example, if a commercial bank is located on a state line, its 4-C8 nonbanking subsidiaries can operate in surrounding states, while its branches can only operate physically within the home office state, and often only within the home office county. Note: regardless of the size of the bank holding company or the state in which it is incorporated, these activities have been permitted by the Federal Reserve System as nonbanking activities. These activities have been considered to be so closely related to banking as to be a proper incident thereto. It should also be noted that these activities can be carried on worldwide, not just within the more restricted geographical boundaries normally used.

Every banker should analyze the opportunities available as a part of the strategic planning process, to determine whether a bank should be reorganized as a one-bank holding company in order to take advantage of some of these 4-C8 activities. These nonbanking activities will continue to expand and it's likely that more new banking powers will be granted to bank holding companies than to commercial banks.

Summary

The purpose of this chapter has been to indicate the significantly changing financial structure and environment in which the banker must operate. Nothing in this chapter has been startling. It has been simply an exploration of the many changes that have taken place in the commerical banking industry over the past five years. These changes will continue to take place, and as they do occur, your job as a banker will continue to become increasingly more complex and more risky than it has been in the past. Strategic planning for

Figure 2-4   Permissible Nonbank Activities for Bank Holding Companies under Section 4(c)8 of Regulation Y

Activities Permitted by Regulation	Activities Permitted by Order	Activities Denied by the Board
1. Extensions of credit[2] Mortgage banking Finance companies: consumer, sales, and commercial Credit cards Factoring	1. Issuance and sale of travelers checks[2, 6] 2. Buying and selling gold and silver bullion and silver coin[2,-][4]	1. Insurance premium funding (combined sales of mutual funds and insurance) 2. Underwriting life insurance not related to credit extension
2. Industrial bank, Morris Plan banks, industrial loan company	3. Issuing money orders and general-purpose variable denominated payment instruments[1, 2, 4]	3. Sale of level-term credit life 4. Real estate brokerage (residential)
3. Servicing loans and other extensions of credit[2]	4. Futures commission merchant to cover gold and silver bullion and coins[1, 2]	5. Armored car 6. Land development 7. Real estate syndication
4. Trust company[2] 5. Investment or financial advising[2]	5. Underwriting certain federal, state, and municipal securities[1, 2]	8. General management consulting 9. Property management
6. Full-payout leasing of personal or real property[2]	6. Check verification[1, 2, 4]	10. Computer output microfilm services
7. Investments in community welfare projects[2]	7. Financial advice to consumers[1, 2]	11. Underwriting mortgage guaranty insurance[3]
8. Providing bookkeeping or data processing services[2]	8. Issuance of small denomination debt instruments[1]	12. Operating a savings and loan association[1, 5]
9. Acting as insurance agent or broker primarily in connection with credit extensions[2]	9. Arranging for equity financing of real estate	13. Operating a travel agency[1, 2]
10. Underwriting credit life, accident, and health insurance	10. Acting as futures commissions merchant	14. Underwriting property and casualty insurance[1]
11. Providing courier services[2]	11. Discount brokerage 12. Operating a distressed savings and loan association	15. Underwriting home loan life mortgage insurance[1]
12. Management consulting to all depository institutions	13. Operating an Article XII Investment Company	16. Investment note issue with transactional characteristics
13. Sale at retail of	14. Executing foreign banking unsolicited	17. Real estate advisory services

Figure 2-4   (*continued*)

Activities Permitted by Regulation	Activities Permitted by Order	Activities Denied by the Board
money orders with a face value of not more than $1000, travelers checks, and savings bonds[1, 2, 7]	purchases and sales of securities	
14. Performing appraisals of real estate[1]	15. Engaging in commercial banking activities abroad through a limited purpose Delaware bank	
15. Issuance and sale of travelers checks	16. Performing appraisal of real estate and real estate advisor and real estate brokerage on nonresidential properties	
16. Arranging commercial real estate equity financing		
17. Securities brokerage		
18. Underwriting and dealing in government obligations and money market instruments	17. Operating a Pool Reserve Plan for loss reserves of banks for loans to small businesses	
19. Foreign exchange advisory and transactional services	18. Operating a thrift institution in Rhode Island	
20. Futures commission merchant	19. Operating a guarantee savings bank in New Hampshire	
21. Options on financial futures	20. Offering informational advice and transactional services for foreign exchange services	
22. Advice on options on bullion and foreign exchange		

[1] Added to list since January 1, 1975.
[2] Activities permissible to national banks.
[3] Board orders found these activities closely related to banking but denied proposed acquisitions as part of its "go slow" policy.
[4] To be decided on a case-by-case basis.
[5] Operating a thrift institution has been permitted by order in Rhode Island, Ohio, New Hampshire, and California.
[6] Subsequently permitted by regulation.
[7] The amount subsequently was changed to $10,000.
Source: *Interstate Banking: Probability or Reality?* David D. Whitehead, Economic Review, Federal Reserve Bank of Atlanta, March 1985. Page 10.

your bank is one way by which you can face the increased uncertainty, risk, and increased competitive pressures while providing a simple rate of return for your investors and insuring corporate perpetuity. Without strategic planning, you will be lost in a sea of cross currents, and the riptide may get you before you have the opportunity to bob to the surface to find which direction your bank must take.

3

How to Begin the Planning Process

Benefits of Comprehensive Commercial Bank Planning

Why Plan?

Your bank should consider preparing a formal comprehensive strategic plan because banks that do plan generally grow faster and make more money. As a result both management and shareholders maximize their return; management in a compensation and personal growth sense, shareholders in a return on investment sense. In addition, it is easy to see why every bank should have a formal, comprehensive corporate plan. The end results of formal planning— explicit, written-out, specific objectives; control mechanisms, and a backup contingency plan—give all parties involved a clear understanding of the future of the bank.

Involve Key People

It is important to keep one fact in mind at the very beginning. Only people who are involved in drafting a comprehensive plan are going to try their best to make the plan succeed. Therefore, the key is managerial involvement. Nothing flatters people more than being taken seriously. In addition, the process of involving management in formal planning improves communication, thereby pulling management together as a team. Finally, planning *is* managing. Formal planning is one of the best ways to develop managerial skills.

Hierarchy of Plans

Planning must be comprehensive to achieve maximum benefits. The strategic plan outlines the general means for achieving the objectives set by the bank. This is quite different from the operating plan which comes from the strategic plan. The operating plan tells you what to do today.

Most banks have (or better have) a written operating plan that guides day-to-day bank activities. The operational plan is a recipe for action; it tells what gets done, who does it, and when. It should be tactical in nature and should be restricted to fine-tuning what the bank is already doing.

Strategic planning, on the other hand, involves looking into the future and deciding what the basic thrust of your bank *ought* to be. It may result in a strategy that over time brings about fundamental changes in your bank's business. The point of strategic planning is to decide a course *today* that will get the bank where it wants to be *tomorrow*.

Prerequisites for Successful Strategic Planning

Experiences in a number of commercial banks have shown that the following points, *all* of which are basic to successful strategic planning, need to be present, understood, and implemented.

It is important to involve functional area managers in the planning process. Managers generally understand their areas better than anyone else. This practical knowledge is critical for the long range planning process. It keeps planning down to earth. In addition, these are the people who will carry out the strategy, and the plan's success depends on their cooperation. They are far more likely to be enthusiastic over a strategy that they've had a hand in making.

The involvement of the president or CEO is also essential. Lip service is *not* enough. Unless the president or CEO is deeply involved in making plans, which may change the thrust of the organization, he or she will not approve them. Besides, deciding the future direction of the bank is the president's job.

It is also important to make time for strategic planning. You can't wait to strategically plan until you have time available. If you do it will never get done. Time requirements are another reason why the CEO must actively lead the planning efforts. If the responsibility for strategic planning is delegated to someone else, it will soon become evident to everyone else that the president or CEO rates strategic planning as unimportant.

Strategic planning also must be integrated with operational planning. The transition from short range plans must be gradual. Few banks can successfully operate with one orientation today and an entirely different one tomorrow. In addition, some short range commitments simply need to be met. If they are not you may lose your power to act. On the other hand, it is important to be thinking of the future. Consequently, it is usually best to develop operational and strategic plans concurrently. Short term requirements may force you to modify your long term strategic plans and vice-versa.

The strategy must be flexible. Strategy can be defined as a bank's reaction to its economic, social, and political environment, both as it is at present and as the bank expects it to be in the future. There is little the bank can do to affect the environment; on the other hand, it does have control over its own response. Therefore, the trick is to determine what the future will be like, and then devise the strategy that enables the bank to operate successfully and profitably within it. However, forecasting skills often leave much to be desired. Therefore, it is necessary to develop a strategy that has sufficient flexibility to succeed in a number of plausible future environments.

Strategic plans must also be constantly reassessed. Don't expect to develop the strategic plan and put it in the vault. Plans must be checked and rechecked and updated to accommodate the unpredictability of the banking/financial services environment. Banks that successfully engage in long range planning examine their strategy at least once a year as a regular part of their normal planning cycle. And the plans are adjusted on an ad hoc basis when critical elements of the environment turn out miles away from the forecast.

Don't look for the universally ideal method of planning; it doesn't exist. No single method of planning applies to all commercial banks. What works best for a single bank depends on basic factors such as the approach (by the numbers or shirt sleeve); size; data; time and staff available to determine how sophisticated the planning will be; and management.

Don't think that you must do everything right the first time. This is one of the greatest pitfalls for commercial banks just starting this strategic planning process. As a consequence, they get bogged down in one or several steps. They never get through the planning cycle in time; sometimes they even give up.

Accept the fact that your first time through will produce only a rudimentary guide to action. Experience indicates that it usually takes at least five years to develop sophisticated plans; however, the benefits from even a rudimentary plan can be great.

You should start the planning process *right now*. If you think it's too late in the year, why not run through the steps in a very general way; taking only a few days. By doing this you will have a better feel for your strategic direction, and thus improve the focus of your short range plan. You will also gain practice, making the planning cycle more productive and easier the second time around. You will have made a commitment, making it less likely that comprehensive planning will be put off another year or until it's too late.

The Planning Process

The steps in the planning process are as follows:

1. Establish objectives, missions, and policies.
2. Conduct a situation analysis.
3. Formulate strategy.
4. Develop the operational plan.
5. Plan for implementation and control.

Organizing for Planning—The Team

The planning team should consist of the bank's top management. It is important to keep the team to eight members or less. More will make it unwieldly, hindering participation and generally making it hard to get things done. At some banks it is obvious who should be on the committee or committees. At others, where the situation is much more fuzzy, membership must be worked out with great care. It is important to keep in mind that since the planning team is one of the most important committees within the bank, some people may take it badly if they're not included. Therefore, here are three broad guidelines:

1. Normally the team should consist of the top management—those officers who report directly to the CEO. If more than seven people report to the CEO, perhaps too many are reporting to him or her, thereby cutting down his or her efficiency. Why not consider reorganizing as a part of setting up your planning team?

2. Is there someone who can make a valuable contribution, but is not a member of top management? If this is the case, restructuring may be in order.

3. If you dip below top management, can you afford to include every-

body on the next management level? If not, who's going to feel hurt that he or she was left out? Do you really want to keep such people in your bank? You should probably ask the same question about someone with high rank whom you'd prefer to leave off the committee.

The President or CEO should chair the planning committee. This will help underscore the importance of the planning team. If someone else serves as chairperson, he or she should be unusually important to the bank or be heir apparent to the CEO. The main advantage of the planning team is that it provides an orderly forum for members of top management to have "their day in court." This boosts morale. People appreciate the chance to present their own ideas and, at the very least, it also makes them more receptive to those of other people. Also, the interchange of ideas usually stimulates great creativity, while the bank-wide experience of committee members keeps the plan realistic.

The final decisions should be made by the chairperson of the committee (President or CEO). He or she must be careful to encourage creative dissent during the meetings. The value of discussions diminishes drastically when members feel it is pointless or unwise to present ideas the chair ignores or disagrees with. Similarly, it is up to the chairperson to make sure a quick or overly aggressive individual doesn't push everybody else to the sidelines.

Drawbacks

The major drawback to the planning team is that often committee meetings seem to be unproductive. Why the bank's highest paid officers are tied up in a committeee meeting, when so much needs to be done out in the bank, is a common gripe. Yet a well run committee may be the most productive way to gain satisfactory results.

To avoid tying up executives unnecessarily, subcommittees made up of planning team members whose function might be to evaluate acquisitions or branches may be used. These ad hoc task forces usually include only those members needed to gather information or analyze data.

How much the planning team members need to know is a common question usually raised by bank presidents. What should be revealed to key employees is a matter of personal choice. The decision boils down to weighing the benefits of involving others versus the loss of secrecy. The alternative may be doing *all* of the planning yourself. There's a general agreement that if you want others to be active on the planning team, they have to know the bank's objectives, financial strengths and weaknesses, past successes and failures.

Area managers often lack the time, patience, and aptitude for formal planning. A possible solution to this problem is for managers to utilize some of the people who report to them. There is no need for managers to do routine work. Have subordinates gather information for the situation analysis so management can restrict their own participation to analysis, strategic discussions, and decisions.

It's also a good idea to at least consider the use of a planning coordinator. Many banks have found that designating someone to coordinate the planning process reduces the work of the chairperson and other team members. The title may vary: it might be planning coordinator, director of corporate planning, or some other title. The person's duties usually include recommending the planning format, scheduling meetings, keeping minutes, helping to gather data, assembling the plan and distributing the plans. He or she is usually a non-voting ex-officio member of the team. It is generally accepted that the coordinator's role is not to develop plans but to facilitate the process.

However, do not underestimate the requirements of the job. A good planning coordinator should have a thorough understanding of the bank and its operations. He or she should have a close working relationship with the president and the respect of its operating managers. He or she serves as a catalyst in the planning process.

Managers should view the coordinator as someone available to them, not as a watchdog who will turn them in as soon as something goes wrong. The coordinator must not be responsible for seeing that the plans are carried out. The coordinator who must report to the president that the performance of one of the operating managers isn't up to snuff loses the trust of that manager and others as well. Who can remain open with the potential executioner? However, it should be noted that most smaller banks cannot afford a full time coordinator. They compromise by using a part time coordinator, usually an individual with a smaller list of other responsibilities.

Consultants should not do your strategic planning for you. They should be used to suggest planning procedures, to provide data for information, (such as competitive data to evaluate the feasibility of particular plans) and to undertake a situation analysis (to eliminate intrabank bias.) Consultants should serve in an advisory or facilitating capacity. The managers must do the planning.

Another common concern is the role of outside directors. This depends upon the nature of the board. Some boards are nothing more than rubber stamps. Others play a much more active role. At the very least your Board of Directors should: 1) help formulate and approve objectives; 2) be briefed on the results of the situation analysis; 3) be briefed and respond to environmental forecasts; and 4) be briefed and respond to strategy development and annual plans.

Steps in the Planning Process in Detail

There are essentially five steps in the planning process.

1. Establish objectives, missions, and policies.
2. Conduct a situation analysis.
3. Formulate strategy.
4. Develop the operational plan.
5. Plan for implementation and control.

Establish Objectives, Missions, and Policies. Before you can do any type of planning, you must decide what you want your bank to be. This means establishing your objectives, missions, and policies. Objectives are usually determined first. However, keep in mind that all are interrelated.

After you have decided who is on the planning team, the first step is to set objectives. The terms goals and objectives will be used interchangeably. Make sure the objectives don't sound like this: a) to maximize profits; b) to produce profits in order to return shareholders adequate dividends; c) to have ample dollars for long term investment.

Who could argue with these vague objectives? They are vague enough to mean all things to all people. That's precisely what's wrong with them.

To construct meaningful objectives first, determine a planning horizon—how far in the future you wish to plan. No single time span is proper. Five years is about the longest time period that is realistic. It is far enough away to make strategic changes in the plan and not so far away that it makes it unrealistic. After you have decided on objectives for the end of the planning horizon, you should determine objectives for the first year.

Some hints for setting successful objectives are: 1) Set objectives with minimum process restrictions. Allow for flexibility. Make objectives specific. It is obviously easier to agree on broad objectives than on specific ones. Don't waste your time. 2) Make sure that objectives promote unity and purpose so that everyone knows what must be accomplished. 3) Make sure the objectives are measurable. Measure is the key word, because a specific objective is concrete and measurable, whether in dollars, percentages, or proportions. 4) Maximizing profit by itself is not a specific objective.

Be sure to establish an objective for each key area. Make sure an objective for each key area in the bank is concretely defined. Objectives for key areas help avoid ones that are overly broad. A word of caution here however; establish objectives only in key areas. Lengthy lists are impractical.

General headings for key areas could include profitability, growth, dividends, stability or risk, and relative ranking. Specific areas where objectives could be set are noted below. Set objectives on a net dollar basis, a percent increase basis or as a percent of assets, when relevant.

Income/Expense
1. Interest income
2. Interest expense
3. Net interest margin
4. Trust income (if applicable)
5. Service charge on deposits
6. Other non-interest income
7. Salaries and benefits
8. Occupancy, furniture, equipment expense
9. Loan loss provision
10. Tax provision
11. Return on assets
12. Return on equity

Yields and Rates
1. Tax equivalent yield-earning assets
2. Yield on investment securities
3. Yield on loans
4. Net charge off as a % of average loans
5. Rate on total interest earning funds
6. Interest expense as a % of earning assets

Capital Position
1. Effective tax rate
2. Cash dividend (both $ and % income)
3. Capital formation rate
4. Equity capital % assets

Productivity
1. Earning assets as a % of assets
2. Non-interest/cash as a % of assets
3. Personnel expense/employee

4. Employees per million $ assets
5. Non-interest income as a % of salaries

Use of Funds
1. Investment securities
2. Total loans
3. Real estate loans
4. Commercial/industrial loans
5. Personal loans
6. Agriculture/lease financing/other loans
7. Above 6 - % yield, % total; growth in each (% and $)

Sources of Funds
1. Demand deposits
2. Public funds
3. Total demands
4. Savings deposits
5. Time deposits
6. Total time/savings
7. Money markets
8. Time over $100M
9. Above 8 - % cost, % total earning assets; growth in each (% and $)
10. Asset - liability gap

Growth Statistics
1. Income before security transactions (1, 5-yr.)
2. Net income (1, 5-yr.)
3. Average assets (1, 5-yr.)
4. Dividends
5. Growth versus local banks, savings & loan associations, credit unions, non-bank competition, region, state, national
6. Growth versus peer group
7. Market share within county (region) in all key areas; total deposits; demand; savings; total loans; commercial; industrial; mortgage; installment; income; service charges

Non-Financial
1. Marketing/public relations
   a. New products
   b. Product pricing

2. Structure of the board of directors
3. Company characteristics

It is important to make the objectives that you are setting exciting and believable. You should probably shoot for somewhere between probable and impossible. The bank that sets up uninspiring objectives invites a potentially fatal case of passivity in its employees. On the other hand, absurdly high objectives are just as bad. It does little good to establish objectives at a high level if no one really believes the bank can achieve them. Where then, should the bank set its goals? Frederick R. Kappel, former AT&T chairman best responded by noting "Part of the talent or genius of the goal setter is the ability to distinguish between the possible and the impossible—but willing to get very close to the latter."[1]

It's important to gather comparable data in other banks and yours to serve as a reference point, and to plot past performance versus a trend line for the future. Part of the genius of top management is to convince everybody that they *can* rise to the challenge.

It's also important to rank objectives in the order of importance. When you can't decide order, use this procedure. Place the objectives in two groups: must objectives and need objectives. The must objectives are absolutely essential. These are to be obtained at all costs. They have to be reached. Concentrate on these. For example a minimum capital to asset ratio is a must objective. Determine a minimum level of performance for each must objective. Anything else is a need objective. Isolate these and put them on a second tier. Spend your time on the must objectives and then, if you have time left over, concentrate on the need objectives.

It is also very important to commit your objectives to writing. The act of transferring an idea to paper is the first test of its worth. It's amazing how many flashes of inspiration fail this initial test. Also, committing objectives to paper focuses on a specific objective. If objectives are in writng, one can easily compare actual to desired performance and a prominent place in the corporate plan tends to reinforce the original commitment.

Also keep in mind that the objectives are subject to revision, *constant* revision. Objectives set today may become obsolete tomorrow, for one reason or another. If environmental conditions change, you need to allow for the flexibility to change your objectives. An annual or semi-annual review of your objectives will help.

After you have set objectives, specify the mission. The mission takes up broad areas of business where the bank can, or perhaps cannot, operate. In other words, the mission decides the playing field.

A carefully expressed mission statement helps narrow the search for suitable strategies by indicating what areas of business are acceptable. After conducting a situation analysis (which is the next step) and examining the environment, you may revise the mission. The mission is not cast in concrete. It expresses the philosophy of an evolving institution. It should be narrow enough to pinpoint specific areas of concentration but broad enough to allow for creative growth.

Now that you have decided what the bank should accomplish (objectives) and what type of activity the bank should or should not engage in (mission) the next step is to determine corporate policies. These are the rules of behavior that govern top management's behavior, both within the bank and with other banks, financial institutions, and the general public.

Whereas the mission stakes out the playing field, policies specify the rules of the game. Policies delineate courses of action that are acceptable to the bank and, like the acknowledgement of the mission, help focus the search. Policy statements need not be elegant. A policy deserves, however, to be put in writing. This saves time, improves communications, and clarifies murky areas of action. To be effective, policies must be narrow enough to govern managerial activity without obstructing individual initiative and creativity.

You now have the steps to begin the process. You should be able to set objectives, a mission, and policies in several meetings. One guiding rule: don't initially strive for perfection. Remember, objectives tell you what you want to accomplish. A mission tells you what areas of business are acceptable. And policies tell you what rules of conduct are permissible.

How to Conduct a Situation Analysis

Corporate plans are based on assumptions about banks' strengths and weaknesses. It makes sense that the accuracy of your assumptions, in large part determines the effectiveness of your strategy. It is important to undertake a thorough appraisal of your bank. This appraisal of your bank will point out strengths, which can be capitalized on for internal expansion, diversification, or both. Weaknesses, unless corrected, signify that certain strategies should be avoided.

Surprisingly, most banks have no idea what makes them successful. The situation analysis is a diagnostic, in-depth evaluation of an organization—focusing on the strengths and weaknesses of its organizational structure, personnel, and performance on a department-by-department basis.

The rationale for doing a situation analysis is to enhance corporate planning efforts that must be based on the available resources of an organization. It is necessary for every organization to evaluate its own strengths and weaknesses from time to time. Strengths in an organization must be capitalized on to their fullest extent in order for the organization to expand, enter new markets, and increase profitability. The weaknesses of an organization must be identified in order to avoid certain strategies until problems are corrected or the function is amended. Therefore, the situation analysis is the key tool and serves an important function in the strategic planning process.

It is critical to conduct a situation analysis that examines every functional area of the bank. The members of the planning team should take an active role in the analysis. This helps to increase their understanding of the bank. It's important to let the staff assemble the data but make the managers determine what data is gathered then analyze it and coordinate the final report.

In time a situation analysis may be one of the few areas where it would be appropriate to use an outside consultant to assist in the planning process. If you feel it's impossible to get an unbiased report, it may be wise to use an outside consultant to undertake this type of activity.

You can avoid having the situation analysis get bogged down. The idea/process is listed below. It's important to keep a couple of things in mind.

1. Keep the task manageable.
2. Set up a timetable and decide at the outset when it must be completed (roughly two months). Set up timetables for each task, and note the person responsible for each task. If you allow people a nebulous period of time to complete a job, you will invite and probably will get, procrastination. Finally, adhere to the timetable.
3. Keep the situation analysis relevant. Limit your study to information that suggests action.
4. Decide what should be analyzed. No single format fits all banks. However, make sure an analysis of absolute strengths and weaknesses is presented.
5. Devise forms in advance. Have area managers prepare forms that are appropriate for the individual areas *before* you start gathering data. The forms force you to think about what you are going to do, before you start doing it. In addition, it is easier to delegate routine chores of gathering information with forms. Forms serve one other very important function—they tend to eliminate distortions. Since managers are conducting their own analysis, it may be difficult to be objective. You

can avoid a self-serving situation by presenting, discussing, and revising forms at a planning meeting before any information is gathered.

Assuming that you have devised your forms and are beginning a situation analysis, it is important to analyze available secondary information first. As noted in Chapter 5, there are numerous sources available to the analyst.

A sample situation analysis could follow this general format:

1. The planning team sets up a timetable for completion of major steps and a completion date for the situation analysis.
2. Each of the functional areas to be analyzed prepares forms.
3. Each of the functional areas presents sample forms at the planning meeting. The forms are accepted as is, or revised, and at some point in the future are accepted.
4. Each functional area should undertake its own situation analysis, ending up with a one-page summary, supported with necessary documentation. These are then circulated to planning team members for review.
5. Functional areas present their analysis at a planning team meeting. The planning team discusses each separately; accepts and/or revises where necessary.
6. The planning team then hammers out a general agreement of the bank's strengths or weaknesses. This is then consolidated into a one-page summary.

Strategy Formulation

At this point you've determined objectives, missions, and policies; and examined the strengths and weaknesss of the bank. You are now in a position to forecast the future environment in which your bank will operate.

The future is becoming increasingly difficult to pin down. To do this, measure your strategies against several possible future environments. This method produces several key benefits. It enables you, even forces you, to see how a strategy might fare in the event of an unexpected (but possible) future. It also forces you to commit alternatives to paper, helping you clarify assumptions and variables, and hence the logic of your arguments.

To incorporate multiple futures into strategic planning determine the factors relevant to your bank that you are *sure* will occur within your planning timeframe (i.e., assumptions). Then list the uncontrollable variables that could have a make or break consequence on your bank. You then need to assign a range of reasonable values to each key variable and develop at least two but not more than four plausible futures in which your bank could find itself operating (one would be the most probable, worst case, best case, etc.). It is important then to develop the strategy for each future, concentrating your effort on the most probable scenario.

To get the job done it's important to keep the assumptions relevant. It is also important to list the key variables, omitting variables with low probability of occurrence or low potential impact. In addition, consider the timeliness of each variable and try to omit disastrous events as much as possible. Then assign a reasonable value to each key variable. Refer to the sample list of areas where assumptions can be set.

ASSUMPTIONS

General Economy
1. Interest rates
2. Inflation
3. Taxes
4. Industrial base
5. Unemployment

Legislative, Regulatory, Political, and Social
1. Change in core banking legislation
2. Interstate banking—Yes? No?
3. State banking laws
4. Deregulation
5. Political turnover
6. Consumer wants
7. Cash management

Market Trends
1. Convenience versus returns
2. Mergers/Acquisitions
3. Customer targets
4. Age of customers
5. Pricing-competitive
6. "Look alike" financial institutions

Technology
1. Cost
2. Productivity

3. Profitability
4. Reduced price

Human Resources
1. Available/shortage
2. Salary/benefit expense—increases
3. Skill levels needed
4. Cross selling
5. Leisure time

The next step is to describe a number of plausible futures. Concentrate on the most probable case value of each variable, and as a result, come up with the most probable case future. Write from a viewpoint of someone standing in the future. Try to limit yourself to one or two paragraphs and make sure the multiple futures are significantly different from each other.

If possible, try to hold these types of meetings away from the bank. It allows you to brainstorm and be unaffected by the environment of having to work in the bank.

Next, develop a strategy for each scenario. Each strategy should take into account knowledge of future external environments, knowledge of the bank (which you now have based on the situation analysis being completed) and a knowledge of the options available.

Finally, be sure to conduct a preliminary evaluation of each strategy. Is it satisfactory? If the answer is yes, move to implementation of the strategy. If the answer is no, amend and develop a tentative strategy. It's important to continue this process until you obviously answer "Yes!"

How do you put it all together?

1. Set time limits for each step of strategy development. A schedule in writing prevents procrastination from occurring.
2. Review the previous steps. Keep in mind that objectives determine what the bank intends to accomplish and that a mission policy helps keep the search within reasonable bounds. A situation analysis provides a starting point by providing an understanding about the bank's strengths or weaknesses. An environmental analysis depicts plausible future environments.
3. Make a final check of the tentative strategy. Does it do what you want it to do? Is it consistent with the style and philosophy of management? Is there an ample supply of resources? Capital? Personnel? Are the payoffs commensurate with the risks? Is there adequate time for implementation?

Also make sure that you develop (or at least think about) a contingency plan at this point in the process. This is normally developed after a strategy has been finalized, but you should consider it as an integral part of the strategy development. 1) Try to keep the contingency plan as simple as possible. 2) How does one know when the contingency plans should be put into action? Set trigger points, an occurrence which has sufficient impact to cause the contingency plan to be implemented. Be sure to set a trigger point for each key variable. The plan should be simple. It's a reaction. Consider positive as well as negative trigger points in your planning process. In addition, estimate funding necessary for implementation of the contingency plan as part of the planning process.

At this point, introduce your financial people in the discussion. Make rough calculations on a microcomputer for each scenario that you have set up. Make sure you work up cash flow projections in terms of assets, deposits, profits, capital, and cash flow. You can modify your goals based on the results of your planning process. Finally put the strategy in writing. It should be typically no more than five pages.

Developing the Operational Plan
The operational plan is a plan that decides what is to be accomplished; when it should be done; and at what cost. Set up control points and methods of monitoring. The operational plan involves three steps: 1) the detailed operational plan; 2) a pro forma of balance sheets/income statements; and 3) adjustments.

It is important to keep the operational plan as short as possible in each area of the bank. In addition, try to keep it as standardized as possible.

It is important to develop pro forma balance sheets and income statements as part of the operational plan. This is essentially the entire budgeting process and should be based on inputs from all functional areas.

A variance analysis should be included as part of the budgeting process. Obviously, a microcomputer will allow you flexibility to complete this type of analysis.

Finally, adjustments are a critical part of the operational plan. The plan must be constantly reviewed to compare actual versus projected performance and to make it effective.

Planning for Implementation and Control
The final step in the planning process is to plan for implementation and control. Most of the work has been done by this point. The process has three major steps: 1) document responsibilities; 2) set up responsibility charts; and 3) set up activity schedules.

The end result of the process will provide the CEO and each manager with a set of objectives, responsibilities, and activity schedules. These three major steps are analyzed in order.

1. *Document responsibilities.* It is important to spread out key objectives in each of the functional areas. It is also important to communicate their key objectives to the area managers. Keep in mind that each of the area managers should have played an important part in determining what the key objectives are and, therefore, the objectives at this point should not come as a surprise.

2. *Set up responsibility charts.* Each responsibility chart should have an objective, a program, a sub-objective, and critical assumptions listed on it.

3. *Set up activity schedules.* Each executive in the bank should have a schedule to know what is expected when. This is useful: 1) to monitor the success or failure of the plan; 2) to monitor success or failure of that manager; and 3) to use as reference when putting together next year's plan.

The final step in the planning process is to establish a control mechanism. This is one of the most important but the most typically overlooked steps in the planning process.

Initially, it should be decided what should be monitored. Obviously, the objectives that require the most attention should be monitored on an ongoing basis. It is also as important to recognize in advance that everything in the entire strategic plan can't be monitored. Therefore, eliminate those secondary factors and concentrate your monitoring function on the primary and most important objectives.

Try, as a part of the planning process, to determine benchmarks for acceptable performance. By doing so the bank can establish minimum/maximum standards for each objective, and establish an early warning system to see if disaster is pending. The minimum/maximum standards are by now interwoven into the corporate plan. Finally, decide how often a key variable will be monitored; typically on a quarterly or semi-annual basis.

Notes

[1] Frederick R. Kappel, *Vitality in a Business Enterprise.* New York: McGraw Hill, 1960, p. 37–38.

4

Timetable

Let's assume at the very beginning of our discussion that you are a normal bank wanting to set up a normal strategic plan. Let's discuss what the normal planning cycle for the steps presented in Chapter 3 could look like.

The normal planning cycle for a commercial bank should run one year, for a number of good reasons. The first is that senior management's time is limited. Therefore, if the planning process is stretched out over a year, adequate and thoughtful input from all the senior management planning committee is more likely. Secondly, it's impossible to do step B before step A if step B is contingent upon the results of step A. Some things can't be rushed. Time is needed to gather information, conduct surveys, undertake a situation analysis, and to absorb information. Therefore by utilizing a time schedule of one year, the normal planning process will allow each of these steps to occur.

For the remainder of our discussion we'll assume that the normal planning cycle is one year in length. Indicated below is a sample timetable for a commercial bank, presented on a chronological basis assuming that the planning cycle runs for one year in length.

1. Mid-December — Decide on team members; hold an introductory meeting (no more than 1-1/2 hours) where the CEO explains impor-

tance of process and goals. Distribute copies of an outline of what should be ready for the next meeting.

2. Mid-January — In two meetings, set objectives and policies (about 3 hours); analyze track record and objectives; delegate information gathering, if necessary; and discuss mission and policies.

3. Third week in January — (3 hours); nail down objectives, nail down missions/policies.

4. First week in February — Embark on a situational analysis.

5. First week in   April — Start on an environmental analysis; do it away from the bank in one day; (This requires advanced preparation; try to use outside help to add additional ideas when possible); assign a task force the job of analyzing assumptions and determining variables for each; allow six to eight weeks for task force to come up with findings.

6. By May 15th — task force should circulate findings to team; study until June 1st.

7. June 1st — Go away again for a day to review, amend, and reach a consensus on issues not completely resolved; briefly discuss an industry forecast/strategy formulation; assign another task force to develop projections for a multiple scenario environment; schedule meeting in three weeks.

8. June 21st — do the following: discuss projections for each scenario (chart when necessary); discuss and hash out future courses of actions; be sure to keep vacation schedules in mind for next meeting.

9. Arrive at a tentative strategy by July 31st. It gives you a month to make financial projections, develop a contingency plan and make necessary changes based on the first two steps. Put the strategy in writing by August 31, assign projects to functional areas to begin developing operational plans.

10. By September 15th have functional managers circulate operational plans to each member of the planning team.

11. October 1st — Run pro forma balance sheets, income statements, budgets, etc. Should not take more than a week.

12. October 15th — get the planning team together.

13. Have finance man go over the financial statements and make sure they are distributed prior to the meeting.

14. October 30th — Final adjustments to the financial statements.

15. November and December — Set up detailed programs and budgets within each functional department.

16. January 1 — You are finished!

5
Strategic Planning Statistical Sources

You cannot strategically plan in a vacuum. You need statistics, qualitative and quantitative, which will assist you in determining the future course of your bank. There are numerous data sources available for this purpose. In fact, after you view the situation, you could be swamped by so much data that you will never get your strategic planning process finished.

Hard Copy or Software

Almost all sources of strategic planning statistics are now available on computer tapes or discs as well as in hard copy. In fact, some of the Bureau of Census materials, that will be discussed in detail below, are more readily accessible on disc or tape than they are in print. The question is whether you, as a commercial banker, should order hard copy or software packages to utilize your statistics. This will be a personal decision based upon how much data you need from each particular package and/or source. Database information is available for your microcomputer through a modem and the cost of a phone call. Software program charges are not inexpensive, so know what you are looking for before going on-line. We recommend advance research on the necessary hardware, what the program can provide you and what you will save in both time and money. Keep in mind that use of software packages, either off line or on line, may seem expensive, but in contrast, there are no hidden personnel costs, fringe benefits or research costs to prepare similar data. Over the past two years, we have been able to replace the equivalent of four research assistants with one IBM PC and a modem. There are no specific instructions we can give you on exactly where the cutoff is between hard copy and software packages. Certain areas of your bank may utilize more hard copy (research books, census books, etc.) while other areas such as the investment department or the accounting department, may swing toward software packages. However, by utilizing strategic planning spread sheets, statistical sources, and other sources, you will make your planning process more efficient and less costly.

Keep in mind as we go through the rest of this chapter that some of the sources mentioned are available both in hard copy and on software. Also, if your commercial bank is not located near a major research library, access via the microcomputer modem can provide your small rural commercial bank with its own research library. To summarize, examine both the hard copy and the software components of the statistical sources mentioned in the remainder of the chapter. Both sources can be extremely beneficial to your bank.

Public Sources

By far the most important and most pervasive public statistical planning sources are those prepared by the United States government. The Bureau of the Census, located within the Department of Commerce, the Bureau of Labor Statistics, and the Department of Labor are the most imporant sources for financial information covering economic and demographic aspects of the United States environment and economy. Most of the data is gathered on a ten year basis. Additionally, however, the Bureau of the Census and the Department of Labor provide weekly, monthly, quarterly, yearly, and other time period analyses for planning purposes. Though these sources are the most credible, all planners should keep in mind that many of the statistical results published are statistical models, and are thus subject to acceptable levels of error.

By far the most comprehensive of the government information sources is Bureau of Census material. Of interest to bankers are the comprehensive economic, demographic, financial, and income data for specific areas within the United States. If you know exactly what areas you wish to analyze, such as the county and/or region in which your bank is located, the Bureau of Census statistics are by far the most comprehensive and most reliable data source available to you.

The Bureau of Census materials available to the planner is listed. There is some data that is on tape that is not available in hard copy. Also, the Bureau of the Census continuously increases its offerings to the public in order to attempt to provide additional data for planning purposes.

1. Population trends
2. Population compositions
3. Average household size
4. Medium household income
5. Population per household
6. Income statistics—per capita income, median family income, etc.
7. Unemployment statistics
8. Employment statistics
9. Types of skills and unemployment rates
10. International statistics
11. Wholesale trade
12. Retail trade
13. Rental income statistics
14. Communication patterns
15. Age composition
16. Educational levels
17. Ownership versus trends in housing

In many political jurisdictions, state and local governments have attempted to replicate Bureau of the Census data at a more confined level in order to better plan for state and local projects. The financial planner at your commercial bank should always investigate local, regional, and statewide statistics to assist in your planning process. Many times this data is not compatible with that of the Bureau of the Census data, nor is it updated as often. Furthermore, your planners may have to combine dissimilar data to determine trends, especially growth trends, when looking at local statistics. As a final word, it should be noted that some of this data is not completely reliable. We have found that on a regular basis, although not frequently, some of these local statistics have worked to the benefit of the producers of local statistics. A word of warning for those doing the financial planning—make sure that you use common sense and check the data. There is nothing worse than bad data that is represented in the public domain as good data. This is not an overwhelmingly prevalent problem, but bad data does occur frequently enough so that we recommend protecting yourself against making decisions based on improper data.

The Economic Development Administration (EDA), the Small Business Administration (SBA), and some planning commissions are excellent sources for local, regional, and statewide data. These statistics provide information on local economic development and comparisons between state and local economic and demographic statistics such as population, number of households, employment levels, income levels, etc. These statistics assist the planner in determining the relative strength of his or her banking market in relation to other areas within or outside the state.

The second major source of commercial bank planning statistics are the regulatory agencies. The four major federal regulatory agencies, as well as the state agencies, have an enormous amount of data available to the planner. Financial statistics are available not only on an absolute basis for each commercial bank, but also on a relative basis for the entire banking industry. Much of the information is due to the fact that the commercial banking industry is the most fully disclosed industry in the United States. There is more information available in the public press, annual reports, SEC submissions, and on tape than there is for any other industry in the United States.

The Federal Reserve System, the Office of the Comptroller of the Currency, and the Federal Deposit Insurance Corporation collect and disseminate financial statistics that are available to all financial planners. Member bank operation statistics are available at least yearly through the Federal Reserve District Banks, the Office of the Comptroller of the Currency, and the Federal Deposit Insurance Corporation. Financial statements (call reports and statements) are available from the Federal Deposit Insurance Corporation on computer tape with an approximate 3-4 month lag time. The call reports present quarterly data showing the balance sheet and income statements of commercial banks and mutual savings banks. As of 1984, both call reports and income statements will be on a quarterly basis, thus providing the planner with more timely information about the profitability of competitors. The Federal Deposit Insurance Corporation, the Federal Home Loan Bank Board, and the National Credit Union Administration publish branch statistics on an annual basis. This data indicates the growth and stability of various branches and the depository flows within a geographic area.

Traditionally the federal regulatory agencies publish their own member bank statistics indicating the financial worth, assets and liabilities, and financial performance of their own members. In addition to the member bank operating statistics, the FDIC issues periodic reports on the assets and liabilities of all insured commercial banks and mutual savings banks. The Federal Reserve publishes statistics in the Federal Reserve bulletin and periodically on particular financial matters. The Office of the Comptroller of the Currency has the Small Bank Surveillance System (SBSS) program, designed to catch problem banks early enough to correct problems and forestall failure. National banks can utilize the SBSS system to assist in the improvement of efficiency and to see how they differ from peer group banks.

By far the most comprehensive comparative program, which financial planners have utilized since 1964, is the Federal Reserve Functional Cost Analysis Program. The Functional Cost Analysis Program is an excellent tool for financial planning. However, you have to be a contributor to the functional cost analysis program at your local district Federal Reserve Bank to be able to receive the data. Some data is made public however, but the data that is publicly released is limited compared to the detailed information available to subscribers. So if you want to compare in great detail the functional cost of your bank with those of peer group banks, either locally, or in other similar economic and demographic situations, you must be a member of the functional cost program at your local Federal Reserve district bank.

Using the functional cost program will assist your bank to determine the pricing of products and services in the future, as well as determining the current efficiency of the interest and non-interest expense categories of your financial institution. Considering that the industrial sector of the United States economy has been using cost accounting for over seventy years, it seems somewhat ludicrous to have to discuss the functional cost program in the banking industry. However, the functional cost program system has only been available for the past twenty years, and less than twenty-five percent of the banks in the United States use it. Understanding commercial bank costs needs improvement and the ability to strategically plan for the future will depend upon the ability to understand the cost structure of the bank.

Before leaving the discussion of functional costs analysis, it should be noted that several of the national certified public accounting firms also have a functional cost program which your bank can utilize. Needless to say, you need to be a client in order to be able to receive the data. The only problem with this type of functional cost program is that there would be a small number of banks in the survey.

As a final note to the planner, it is often worthwhile to examine the profitability trends of your bank against that of other financial intermediaries within your marketplace. Statistical data is published by the Federal Home Loan Bank Board System, the National Credit Union Administration and other public sources which give an indication of the depository, asset and liability, and financial performance of non-bank financial intermediaries. As non-bank financial intermediaries become more competitive with your commercial bank, you need to know more about their financial trends to determine your strategic plan. Where non-bank financial intermediaries are important competitors, gather statistics on how they have performed (i.e., profitability, deposit growth, asset and liability management, capital adequacy, and other indicators) so that a comparison can be made between your bank's performance of these non-bank financial intermediaries. The more you know about your competition the more you will be able to financially plan your commercial bank into a survivability mode.

Private Sources of Statistical Information

In addition to the public sources noted, there are a number of private corporations, trade associations, and educational sources that provide financial statistics to financial institutions for purposes of corporate planning.

The most pervasive financial souce is the information provided by the Sheshunoff Corporation, Austin, Texas, which uses computer programs to unscramble the FDIC computer tapes. The books compiled are a wealth of information for those doing competitive analyses within any particular state. Furthermore, the Sheshunoff books indicate the rates of return, five-year historical comparisons, and a ranking of banks by size and performance skill. The Sheshunoff Corporation also provides seminars and performs comparative analyses for individual banks.

Another private source of commercial bank planning information is the Bank Administration Institute (BAI). Bank Administration Institute is an education-oriented banking association located in Rolling Meadows, Illinois. Bank Administration Institute, through its emphasis on financial research and publications, is the outstanding publication and research foundation in the entire financial institutions field. BAI prepares performance ratios for commercial banks in all fifty states at considerably lower cost than the Sheshunoff books. For example in 1984, the BAI service was approximately $695.00 for the entire country, while the Sheshunoff books were $245.00 for the first state plus $195.00 for each additional state.

A data base source of commercial bank financial information is available. Innerline, jointly owned by BAI and the American Banker, has a ratio analysis program in its "on-line" data base service through which bankers can analyze the financial statements of any commercial bank anywhere in the United States.

A final recommended source of planning information and statistics is Decision Research Sciences (DRS). Decision Research Sciences Inc., in Blue Bell, Pennsylvania, publishes a *Branch Directory and Summary of Deposits with Market Indicators*. This comprehensive source book analyzes the growth in deposits of commercial bank offices, savings and loan association offices, mutual savings bank offices, and credit unions. This information is drawn each year from the June 30th FDIC, Federal Home Loan Bank, and National Credit Union Administration computer tapes. This publication does not include financial performance statistics but does indicate the location of other intermediaries and their trends in deposits over a period of time. This branch directory also estimates the deposit pool in certain geographic areas, since it has the ability to aggregate the totals of each of the depository financial institution offices within the market. In addition, Decision Research Sciences publishes data on state levels and aggregates market share data for subcomponents within each state and for the states themselves. It should be noted that these market shares on subregional and state levels are based upon definitions drawn by DRS itself, and not from any federal regulatory agencies and/or the Department of Justice. Therefore, be cautious when using such market share definitions. Overall, however, the material published by DRS has an excellent reputation for quality and is useful to financial planners in their planning process.

Articles, Monographs, Books, and other Research Sources
The financial planner should never forget about articles, monographs, books, and other research materials published by public sources, academic scholars, and professional bankers. These individuals and their institutions support significant research in the development and performance of financial institutions.

There are some major publications that publish regular articles on strategic planning and comparative financial performance which can be useful to you in terms of financial planning. 1) *The American Banker* — Banking's daily newspaper, has articles of current interest and features which include strategic planning and other items. 2) *Magazine of Bank Administration* — A monthly magazine oriented toward operations and financial control which features excellent articles in the area of strategic planning. 3) *The Bankers Magazine* — A quarterly publication published by Warren, Gorham & Lamont, Inc. which also has excellent articles on various planning subjects. 4) *Journal of Bank Research* — A more detailed and theoretical publication with most articles written by academics or federal regulatory economists. 5) *Issues and Bank Regulation* — A relatively recent publication from the Bank Administration Institute which focuses on the major issues facing commercial banking and the whole structure of deregulation of financial intermediaries. 6) *The ABA Banking Journal* - This magazine, published monthly by the American Bankers Association, has many practical articles; many written by bankers. Over the past two years we have found excellent articles on the area of strategic planning in this magazine.

This list is not complete. It does not include such publications as *Banking, Bankers Monthly,* or *U.S. Banker.* These publications are also worthwhile but they seldom have articles on corporate strategic planning. On the other hand, they are excellent sources for the financial planner while analyzing the trends of the financial service industry over the next 5-10 years.

The following is a list of other publications that can assist you in your financial planning.

Public Sources

Federal government (name of publication, publisher, frequency of publication, format, cost if known)
1. Brearau of the Census
2. Bureau of Labor Statistics
3. Department of Labor
4. Securities Exchange Commission (SEC)
5. Federal Reserve System
6. Office of the Comptroller of the Currency (Department of the Treasury)
7. Federal Deposit Insurance Corporation
8. Federal Home Loan Bank
9. National Credit Union Administration

State and Local
1. SBA

Other
1. EDA

Private Sources

1. Sheshunoff
2. Bank Administration Institute

3. Innerline
4. Compuserve

Magazines and Regular Publications

1. Bankers Magazine
2. Magazine of Bank Administration
3. Journal of Bank Research
4. Issues and Bank Regulation
5. Journal of Money Credit and Banking
6. Journal of Commercial Bank Lending
7. ABA Banking Law Journal
8. Banking Law Journal
9. Banking
10. Bankers Monthly
11. US Banker

Summary

The sources of financial information you use in strategic planning are extremely important for your survival as a commercial bank. These sources do have a tendency to be fluid over time and you should pay special attention to the development of new sources which will assist you in the improvement of your strategic planning.

By far the most important improvement in the area of source information is the significant amount of public and private data which is now available on disc, over the line through your microcomputer modem. The sources for your strategic planning information will not diminish in the years to come. You will have to pay particular attention to sifting out that information which will be relevant to your commercial bank while ignoring nonrelevant information. However, it may be impossible to prepare the long term goals and objectives of your commercial bank and then to budget short-term, without taking into consideration all of the public and private sources of information which give you the environment in which to do it.

6

Long Term Strategic Planning

We have chosen to discuss long term strategic planning before discussing short term planning, since the short term strategic plans are a series of short and intermediate term plans which fit into the overall goals and objectives of the commercial bank's long term plan. If you have not established a long term strategic plan, then a series of short term strategic plans, whether or not they are of any value, will not result in any satisfaction of long term goals and objectives. Therefore, we shall commence with an analysis of long term strategic planning goals and objectives, and then in Chapter 7 show how these long term goals and objectives can be met over time by successful short term strategic planning.

Independence or Sell Out

By far the most important goal or objective that must be decided by the Board of Directors of your community bank is whether to continue to operate as an independent entity, or to sell out. As discussed in Chapter 2 economic and financial conditions are changing rapidly in the commercial banking industry, and many Boards of Directors are faced with the question of whether to continue to operate the commercial bank, or on behalf of the shareholders to sell out and to turn an illiquid investment into a liquid asset.

It is not our role to suggest that you as the bankers and Board of Directors either operate as an independent or sell out. However, it is our responsibility to bring to your attention as strongly as possible that the long term strategic goals and objectives of your institution will be impacted greatly by your decision to continue to operate as an independent entity, or to plan to sell out either in the next year or over the short term. Please keep in mind that to continue to operate as an independent entity does not prohibit you from selling out if conditions change. On the other hand, selling out a financial institution is a decision which once made is irrevocable, unless the transaction is not approved by the responsible regulatory authority or by your shareholders. Thus, if your community bank decides to remain independent, you must know all the problems and uncertainties that independent operation will bring to bear, and your shareholders should be apprised of the increasingly complex and competitive environment in which you will operate. As long as your shareholders and your directors are in concert concerning this continued independency, it will become a cooperative venture for the shareholders, directors, management, staff, and the public service by your community bank.

In most cases, the Board of Directors and the management of the community bank do not know whether the shareholder's wish to retain ownership or sell out. In recent years, we have assisted many commercial banks throughout the United States in polling their shareholders to find out exactly how they stand on the subject of continued operation versus selling out. There is no absolute guarantee that your community bank will survive.

In almost all cases, you have a legal charter in perpetuity. On the other hand, there is no economic or financial perpetuity guaranteed for your survival. Furthermore, you are custodians of your shareholders' money. The "book value" of your bank, divided per share, is a reflection of the funds invested by your shareholders in your institution. They should have the final say whether to sell out or to continue to operate independently. It is your responsibility to periodically examine the question and find out from your shareholders how they feel on the subject. Obviously, if your shareholders are represented by a majority or two thirds of the shares on the board itself, a comprehensive polling of the remainder of the shareholders may not be necessary. On the other hand, if your Board of Directors represents the shareholders, but does not have more than 15 to 30% of the outstanding stock of your bank held on record or beneficially, then your directors may not reflect the feelings of your shareholders.

Examine your shareholders list carefully. Is it made up of individuals in their 60s, 70s and 80s? What percentage of your shares are held by individuals who have held the stock for 30 to 50 years? How many of your shares are owned by beneficiaries of the original shareholders, and how many of them are located 500 to 2,000 miles away from your bank? Are your shareholders loyal? Will they sell out if they get a price, in spite of the excellent performance of your bank? These questions could go on and on. What is important is that you, as management and the Board of Directors of your community bank, understand that you represent the shareholders, and that the shareholders should make the decisions on a periodic basis whether you continue in business or you look for opportunities to sell out at the highest possible price.

If your bank is typical, the rate of return (dividend yield) that you are yielding to your shareholders on an annual basis is 3-5%. True that is a cash rate of return, and perhaps you are giving them approximately 5-8% on a total rate of return basis. But, they look at alternative investment yielding anywhere from 8-12%, more or less, and may see that their investment is not very good. In addition, note that your stock may be selling significantly below book value, in order to give a realistic rate of return in the marketplace for those shareholders investing today. If the forecast is that conditions won't change materially, your shareholders may desire to sell out the bank, pay their capital gains, and reinvest in a more liquid and higher yielding security. Maybe they will, and maybe they won't. But, can you truly know how they feel without finding out from them on an occasional basis? We recommend that you poll your shareholders every two or three years to see how they feel about the subject of continued operation versus obtaining a more liquid investment through the selling out of the bank to another financial institution.

It's not easy to decide whether to operate as an independent entity or to sell. That's an issue that many bankers try to completely ignore, hoping that it will go away, and hoping that they can continue to make a livelihood without answering the principal question whether the financial institution is meeting its goals and objectives on behalf of the shareholders. Our recommendation is to call a special board meeting, and then discuss absolutely nothing other than the question of whether the bank should continue to operate as an independent entity or sell out.

An optimistic and pessimistic forecast for the future operations of the bank should be gathered prior to the board meeting and disseminated to the directors. Secondly, opportunities to sell out should be examined and possible alternative purchasers who might be interested in the bank should be considered. A deadline for this examination should be established by the board so that it does not interfere with the overall operations of the bank. If one starts to examine this area of continued independence versus selling out, it can completely debilitate the entire institution. Therefore, this fundamental question should be examined thoroughly, but also quickly. Once the time schedule for such examination is outlined, follow it and then make a decision. If the decision is to continue to operate independently, put the entire exercise behind you and move on to the long term and short term planning processes. If the decision is to sell out, then short term strategic planning goals and objectives may be established which will best condition the bank for sale. For example, it is the tendency of buyers to examine the most recent year's performance and to examine the quality of the assets and liabilities at the time of purchase. Therefore, attention can be paid to the improvement of earnings and the improvement in the quality of assets and liabilities in order to sell the bank at a higher price. This is not window dressing as expressed by the regulatory authorities. It is prudent management to attempt to make the bank as saleable as possible in the short term. You must keep in mind that not all commercial banks that sell are in poor financial health. In fact, most purchasers would rather acquire commercial banks that are in excellent health, with competent management, than they would commercial banks for which the regulatory authorities recommend bail outs. Competent bankers are not a dime a dozen, and therefore they are certainly an important part of the overall assets of the selling bank, as much as the quality of loans and securities and the core deposit nature of the liability. Thus, comprehensive attempts to increase the quality of the bank to be sold may be very well rewarded over the short term.

If your Board of Directors decides to sell the bank, it doesn't mean you have to sell it immediately. In fact, if you decide that the bank should be sold in a 3-5 year planning horizon, you have almost three years to improve the quality of the bank prior to the sale. In addition, there may be banking structural restraints in your state that would prohibit the bank from being sold at variable prices over the short term, and permitting you to be able to improve the quality of the performance of the bank so that the bank becomes extremely attractive. The more time you have available, the better off you are. It may be worthwhile for you to examine selling the bank in the 3-5 year horizon because of the age of your major shareholders, the lack of management succession in your bank, or any other conditions that seem prevalent in your area which would not necessitate the sell but would make the sell a very profitable alternative to your shareholders. The more time that you have to plan, the better the price will be assuming that you have increased the value of your bank through improved financial performance. There is one caveat in this whole arrangement, however. That is that as states open up their banking structures to additional alternative forms of merger, consolidation, or acquisition, premiums for banks seem to decline as the commercial banking organizations mature within the states. Alternatively phrased, the first wave of a premium seems always to be higher than the second or third wave.

This is true almost regardless of which state you are talking about. Those who sell out immediately after a major structural change usually get higher premiums than those who wait 3-5 years and then sell out, assuming that the two commercial banks were relatively similar in their performance, size, and location. There will always be "diamonds" regardless of the stage of banking structural change within a state. But, as the states mature after a significant number of mergers and acquisitions, there seem to be more rocks among the diamonds, and premium prices fall as the banks left over for possible acquisition are located in less attractive economic areas, have less profitable previous performance, and often have portfolios whose quality is dubious. Therefore, keep in mind that if you want to sell in 3-5 years, don't talk youself out of a high premium that you could have obtained. It's quite possible that the premium may decline even though the value of your bank has gone up significantly in the 3-5 year horizon. The overall impact on the shareholders will be approximately the same as it would be if you sold out today. And worse, there is the present value loss of the money that the shareholders would have had over the 3-5 year horizon.

Remember Your Fiduciary Duty
Whether you decide to remain independent, or you decide to sell, document all of your deliberations carefully. You never can tell when there will be an irate, unhappy, and vehement shareholder who decides to take you to court. You as the Board of Directors and management of the bank have a fiduciary duty to your shareholders, and one of those duties is to protect their investments. If you have the opportunity to give them significant investment increase (through sale of the bank), and you do not do so, you may be charged with misfeasance or malfeasance. The more you document your deliberations on the question of survivability or sale, the better off you will be if any shareholders decide that you have acted inappropriately. If you simply bring the question up at a board meeting, go around the table, and then make a decision, you probably have not documented the decision-making process in enough detail to protect yourself from harm.

What happens if a legitimate offer comes in from an outside banking organization? This is one of the most paralyzing things that can happen to a

Board of Directors. The Board of Directors likes things simple, without ripples and major floods, tornados or hurricanes, and to have a purchase offer dropped on the table, unsolicited, is an extremely traumatic matter.

If you haven't valued your bank, how do you know what it is worth? If the offer comes in from a legitimate commercial banking organization or individuals, you may be placed in a defensive position which runs contrary to your long term decision to remain independent. How do you know how to respond to the offer? If you have not corresponded with your shareholders, and they are not in concert with you about your future course of operations, the knowledge that such an offer is in existence will place more pressure on you. If you have not valued your bank you quickly will have to run out and get a valuation done by an independent party, and then decide if the offer is adequate, fair, or even outrageously favorable to you.

You may have to poll your shareholders to see if they are interested in selling at that point in time, especially if they know the terms of the offer. If you as directors make the decision not to sell, based upon a legitimate offer, you may have to document your decision. In spite of all the warnings, there are no cases in the law of the United States that have shown that the Board of Directors has failed to meet its fiduciary duty if it has documented its process of examination and determination whether to sell or not, and it has abided by the business judgment rule. However, there are indications that a snap decision based upon little or no deliberation may make the Board of Directors subject to litigation from its own shareholders.

There is no easy way to decide what you should do when an unsolicited offer hits the table. Whatever you do, you should use outside help, operate quickly, examine the entire proposition thoroughly, and make the appropriate decision. It is not unusual for you to discuss the offer with your principal shareholders, especially those who hold enough shares to pass the acquisition through your shareholder base. Often you might indicate via the mass media that you have received such an offer, its general terms, and that you must make a decision. This will give your shareholders an opportunity to let you know quickly and orally how they feel about the offer. If your shareholders do not approve of the offer, regardless of its pricing and terms, you are in a much better position to continue to operate as an independent community bank, regardless of how favorable the offer really is. The major alternative available to the soliciting corporation is to go to the shareholders directly. But, if your shareholders are vehemently opposed to the acquisition, regardless of the pricing, this is not practical. If the potential buyer uses common sense, the offer will simply be withdrawn and another acquisition target sought. However, if you don't know what your shareholders are thinking, and you have not tapped their resources for such information, then the soliciting corporation may simply go right around the Board of Directors and make a tender offer for the shares of your bank directly to the shareholders. Then, you may end up being directors of an institution controlled by someone else and no participation in the changing of the guard. Needless to say, this technique is not always favorable to the directors and management of the target bank after the acquisition has been approved and consummated.

Developing a Mission for Your Bank

If you have decided to remain independent, what is your first responsibility in determining long term goals and objectives?

First you have to develop a mission for your bank. There are approximately 14,500 commercial banks in the United States. Approximately 10,000 of these are still independent, and operate within the fifty states and territories of the United States. Each of these independent commercial banks operates not only as a community bank but also as a corporation, chartered either within the several states or by the federal government through the National Banking Act as supervised by the Office of the Comptroller of the Currency. You are all corporations, similar but different businesses, and you all can develop your own independent missions.

Your mission should define the purpose of your existence. Assuming that you can determine your purpose, how are you going to achieve your goals and objectives?

Figure 6-1 is an illustrative mission for a community bank. It may not be exactly your mission. But, it illustrates how you should develop a mission for your bank. The mission is simply your determination of your own goals and objectives in a general sense. The adoption of such a mission by your Board of Directors and dissemination of such mission to your shareholders is a critical step in planning. The dissemination portion of this entire process is extremely important. It permits your shareholders to know exactly how the bank is planning to proceed over the long term. It does not mean that you are not going to change your mind as conditions change, but at the time of the decision making process you have decided to do this or that for the next 5 to 10 years, and your shareholders should be made aware of what you plan to do. Your shareholders can either then tell you that you are all wet, and cause you to go back and modify your mission, or, if particular shareholders aren't too thrilled about what you are planning to do over the 5 to 10 years, they can always sell out. Either way, your shareholders then are in concert with what the Board of Directors has decided on their behalf, and thus the tripod of importance,

Figure 6-1
STATEMENT OF PURPOSE AND MISSION

It shall be the purpose and mission of this organization to operate a commercial bank and such other activities as permitted by state and/or federal law which are so closely related to commercial banking to be a proper incident thereto. All such activities must be consistent with the purposes and objectives of the shareholders of this organization. It shall be the purpose and mission of this organization to remain an independent entity, to serve our customers, depositors, and friends as efficiently as possible, and to operate within our community to the best of our ability. The community that we shall serve shall be that physical area in which our offices and/or business contacts are such as to provide a network of products and services to the public, and shall not be constrained by artificial barriers such as city, county, or regional boundaries. Over time, our definition of community may change as we have the opportunities to merge and acquire other businesses, but it shall be our purpose and mission to remain an independent entity in contrast to statewide or national branching and bank holding company organizations.

It shall be the mission of this organization to strive to attain the maximum benefit to the investment of our shareholders in terms of both short-term yield and long-term growth. This organization will also attempt to minimize the risk to our shareholders by making prudent business decisions by maintaining adequate levels of capital and reserves.

This bank recognizes the importance of the customers and communities it serves, and will strive to provide the highest level of products and services achievable. Further, it is the objective of this organization to provide such products and services in consistency with our objectives of long-term profitability and maximum shareholder wealth.

management/Board of Directors/shareholders, will all be on the same wave length concerning the future course of the operations of the bank.

A mission statement should be broad enough to encompass all of the alternatives available to the bank. At the same time, it should be specific enough to indicate that the bank is either going to operate independently or sell out; operate as a single unit or branch extensively; look for mergers and acquisitions or not look for them. It should describe in general terms the aspects that a specific series of goals and objectives determined by long term strategic planning will encompass. This mission statement should indicate exactly what the institution's mission is to you and your shareholders.

Furthermore, the mission statement has another impact upon the long term strategic planning process as well as the operation of your bank. Once the mission has been developed, and this is not an easy thing to accomplish, it does permit the Board of Directors, the management, and the staff to operate in a concerted fashion to meet goals and objectives as outlined by the mission statement. Without such a mission statement, it is almost impossible for the bank to develop a cohesive planning process that will be a framework for future financial and operational performance.

Keep in mind that your mission statement is not necessarily the mission statement of your competitor. It may not be the mission statement of any other commercial bank or savings and loan in your community. It is a reflection of what you believe you and your shareholders want for your institution. Thus, it must be developed knowing that it will guide your commercial bank over the long run, or at least the short end of the long run as faced by your institution.

Goals and Objectives

In determining your long range planning, it is absolutely essential for you to form specific and general long term goals and objectives for your bank. In putting together your mission statement, a great portion of this job will be done. However, a mission statement is general by its very nature, and out of your general goals and objectives as reflected by your mission statement, you are going to end up having to specify some of these goals and objectives much more critically in order for management to be able to meet the goals and objectives over time.

As we go through the rest of this chapter, we shall examine some of the essential areas of your bank which must have goals and objectives, both in general and specific context. As we develop this keep in mind that these may not be all of the goals and objectives that you want for your own commercial bank. Each commercial bank is unique so your community bank may be different from somebody else's. Therefore, these are used as examples of how goals and objectives should be outlined for the long term, and how they should impact your ability to perform over the long term. You may have particular areas in which you believe that goals and objectives should be specified for your own management and staff, and if you do, simply use the same techniques for developing those areas not mentioned. Things have changed quickly in the commercial banking industy over the past five years and it is almost impossible to predict what types of strategic planning goals and objectives you should have in 1987 or 1988 in relation to 1984 and 1985. So many new opportunities or challenges may face you that you will need to develop different goals and objectives than you might have had in the past. For example, in 1980 had anybody heard of brokered funds? What is your policy concerning brokered funds? Do you permit brokered funds or not? If you looked at any particular book on devising specific goals and objectives, you might not find anything on brokered funds, because they have come into fashion, famous or infamous depending upon your viewpoint, in recent years. And, they may be gone by the time you have to develop your goals and objectives. Discount brokerage is now available, and it wasn't available prior to 1980. Do you want it? If so, develop a policy on how you are going to operate your discount brokerage. Who knows what's going to be available in 1990? Whatever it is, as it comes along, you should develop a long term objective or goal concerning that particular functional area of your bank. You must decide whether you are going to offer the product or service, and if so, how you plan to offer it, at what prices, and under what conditions.

Thus, goals and objectives of long term strategic planning must be added and deleted as conditions change over time. It will be up to you to make sure that you continue to examine and review these goals and objectives.

We are noting the accountability and review function at this point in order to make you familiar with the fact that all decisions about short term or long term strategic planning are subject to accountability and review. Do not believe that all of the goals and objectives that you have made are so firmly set in concrete that they can never be changed. If you worry so strongly that all of your goals and decisions are firmly decided for the next decade, then you will find yourself in a strategic planning paralysis. If you keep in mind that all decisions are open to accountability and review, and that modifications are a way of life, then bad decisions made by you and the Board of Directors can be counteracted by another decision. Furthermore, it also indicates that as conditions change, you may have to modify or delete various decisions because of the changing conditions. Accountability and review act as a counter balance to the short term and long term strategic planning process. Yet they give you the freedom to make decisions today which can be altered by business judgment decision-making processes in the future.

Profitability Objectives

Profitability is important only to two constituent bodies: your shareholders and the regulatory agencies. If you have decided to remain in business, and operate independently for the foreseeable future, your first major task is to determine your potential profitability standards. This profitability objective must take into consideration not only your maximum potential profit, but also your realistic optimum profit levels based upon restraints imposed upon your operational function by lack of management staff, need for an increase in capital expenditures, and/or any other items that might make the year-to-year operations more expensive than anticipated.

Great quantum leaps in profitability are not achievable year-to-year, but may be so over time. When devising your long term profitability picture, you should determine where you want to be five years from now, and get there slowly. It is impossible to go from a .6% rate of return on assets to 1.5% rate of return on assets in a one-year period of time unless radical surgery is done on bank operations. On the other hand, going from a .6% rate of return on average for the past three years to a five-year running average of 1.4% through significant operational performance improvement and achievement of long term profitability goals might be achievable.

You should know that whether you decide your objectives are a .8% rate of return on average assets or 1.6% rate of return will depend upon the competitive marketplace in which you operate, conditions specifically involving your bank, costs of funds, rates that you can charge on loans, and employee costs involved in the operation of your bank. No two commercial banks are the same. When you analyze what would be your optimum profitability objectives, keep in mind that you have to operate within an individual framework. Although there are all sorts of standardized industry averages such as rate of return on average assets or rate of return on net worth that are published by the Federal Reserve, the Office of the Comptroller of the Currency, the FDIC, and private sources, these averages are simply averages. They do not reflect your personal conditions within your own marketplace. Furthermore, if you believe that a .5% rate of return on assets is necessary for the next five years in order to be able to modernize your bank, upgrade your equipment, hire new employees and train them to be managers, and to improve all other facets of the bank, a .5% rate of return on assets would not be a bad goal or objective. This is in spite of whatever the regulatory authorities would say or your peers would say. This certainly is a more plausible approach to long term strategic planning than to attempt a 1.8% rate of return on average assets out of your bank on a yearly basis. You would end up with such an old banking house that it would have to be blown up and rebuilt. Additionally, you would have to deplete the staff making it inadequate to meet the needs of the community, and pay under market rates on deposits, all for the sake of having a 1.8% rate of return so you can be proud at the next bankers' convention or at least keep the regulatory agencies off your back.

There have always been tradeoffs to survival. One of the major constraints that an independent community bank will have to realize over the next decade is the acceptability of a lower rate of performance in many local markets in contrast to those banks who do not remain independent. In spite of whether there is economy of scale in banking or not, we believe strongly that holding company and affiliate operations, as well as branch banking and local markets, places competitive pressure upon local banks who choose to remain independent. Therefore, by paying higher rates on deposits, and having to charge lower rates on loans, and having to pay industry levels on salaries and wages, there will be profitability pressures placed upon the commercial banks who remain independent. This, however, does not mean that the bank is doomed. The shareholders, management, and the Board of Directors simply have to understand the price that must be paid for being independent and community oriented. There is no magic profitability level. You don't receive a gold ring as the merry-go-round turns every time you hit a 1% rate of return on assets. If your bank has an excellent rating (one or two), has adequate capital, has good liquidity and is well managed, there is no reason why the earnings couldn't be .3% rate of return on all assets or .6%, rather than 1-1/2%, if the difference meant whether you had to sell out or not. Thus, as you are planning your profitability guidelines for the next five years, take into consideration what your marketplace will allow. And, be cognizant of the restraints that you may have as an independent bank operating within the marketplace.

Until now we have not mentioned the rate of return on net worth. This is because we don't believe that standard is as good for measuring improvement as the rate of return on assets. The rate of return on net worth is influenced by the level of capital that each commercial bank has at any one point in time. For example, two commercial banks which earn the same degree of net income at the end of the year may be precisely the same size, but one has twice as much capital as the other. They will have precisely the same rate of return on average asset. But one will have twice as good a rate of return on net worth. The two banks are almost identical except one has stored up capital in the past twice as well as the other. So, the rate of return on net worth for the one which has stored its capital is half as good as the one which has less capital. Others have felt that the rate of return on net worth is an important variable to look at. But, it often is contradictory to the good earnings performance of the commercial bank because of the high or low level of capital adequacy. Therefore, we are much more interested in analyzing the rate of return on average assets to show how the community bank compares with its peers of the same size under similar conditions and without the vagaries of the capital asset ratio.

Phrased another way, if you as bankers and members of the Board of

Directors try to compare your profitability objectives with other commercial banks on the basis of comparing rates of return on net worth, you may mislead yourself as to how profitable you are, or they are. This is simply because of the differing levels of capital adequacy in commercial banks of the same size. This difference could be due to the different operational performance levels, historical capital adequacy levels, dividend payout ratios, and a myriad of other things. However, if you compare your performance with that of other commercial banks based upon a rate of return on average assets, then you can project like matters. The amount of capital adequacy is of no importance, but their ability to make a dollar out of their average assets is the same. Thus, we recommend that you do your projections when analyzing the competition on the basis of rates of return on average assets, and not rates of return on net worth.

A final caveat as we leave this section of the book. Please keep in mind that you should have some profitability guidelines. Whether they are .8% rate of return or 1.5% rate of return is probably less material than having them. Why? Simply because your management needs a point of reference for purposes of determining the efficiency of their operational performance. Profitability guidelines, as shareholders are informed, represent goals and objectives for the management and the Board of Directors. And, at the same time, they act as measuring sticks of efficiency. In addition, if compensation is reflected through bonuses and stock options as well as salary, they can reflect achievement of tangible goals and objectives of profitability. Regardless of what the goals are, they should be determined by the Board of Directors and the management, be achievable, and be announced to the management, the staff and the shareholders so that they do become tangible objectives for all to accomplish.

Capital Adequacy

According to the FDIC, there is never adequate capital. However, the regulatory authorities are going through their third capital adequacy catharsis in four years. Shortly after the Continental Illinois "almost" bank failure, the regulatory authorities revealed new stronger capital adequacy standards, stronger than those they revealed in 1983, which followed those that they had revealed in December of 1981. Catch the pattern! When it comes to capital adequacy, the regulatory authorities have a knee jerk reaction. If a bank fails, especially if it is a large bank, there's a reaction to try to get more capital into all of the banks in the United States, so that less will fail. The ultimate extreme of this absurd theory is to make sure that everybody's 100% capitalized so that no banks will fail. However, the statistics have shown over the past two decades that of banks with 8% capital on average, less fail than if the industry has 7% capital on average, or even 6%. Due to the international risk and uncertainty, coupled with economic recession and past lending experience, the multinational and national banks have been the hardest hit by this latest wave of increased capital adequacy.

You as the commercial banker, in projecting your long term strategic plan, must keep capital adequacy in mind. If there is any financial variable that will come home to roost unfavorably for you, it is capital adequacy. The regulatory agencies, whether they are state or federal, watch capital adequacy like a hawk. Coupled with loan quality, they will place unfortunate and limiting restraints on your operations if your capital adequacy is not kept in line.

Therefore, as you plan for the long term, you should keep as a given the variable of capital adequacy at least at the minimum level, if not higher. For example, if you believe that capital should be at a 7% average level in order to keep the Federal Reserve or the Comptroller off your back in your local market, then all of your projections of growth in terms of assets and deposits income, items such as employees' salaries and dividend payoff, must keep the 7% capital asset ratio in mind. If you do your projections with a 7% capital built in, then you can determine whether you can meet your projections without impinging upon the capital asset ratio and becoming inadequately capitalized during the five-year planning period. If it is impossible to achieve such growth or performance characteristics without impinging upon the capital adequacy income then you realize you have to add capital to your firm in order to be able to meet your objectives. Or, which ought to be obvious, you can always change your goals and objectives to remain capital adequate.

The restraining impact of capital adequacy will often depend upon your ability to raise capital within your local market. If it is impossible, or very hard, to raise capital through common stock floatation, you will have to improve your capital adequacy through floatation of subordinated debentures, or through improved earnings. Some local markets are still very attracted to commercial bank stocks, but most are not. Thus, assuming that common stock sell and the sale of subordinated debentures are not terribly attractive, then capital adequacy has to come through increased earnings retained by your bank. This means that the dividend payout ratio may have to slide as you keep more funds within the bank and that you will have to improve your efficiency in terms of earnings. This might not make your common stock very attractive, since you are keeping the dividends as retained earnings, but it may be your only choice given the conditions of your marketplace. Capital adequacy may be one of the largest problems you have in terms of your long run survival, since it may affect your ability to be able to operate profitably as well as to grow in an increasingly competitive environment.

Let's see how planning for capital adequacy can be impacted by growth in assets and improved operational performance. Figure 6-2 shows that if we projected that assets will grow by 7% from this year's base and that earnings are .60% of average assets and that 75% of all earnings are retained, and also project such growth to take place over the next five years, what impact will it have on the capital of our bank if it is 7.25% at the outset. You will know that over this period of time, if the capital falls below 7%, we would need to infuse capital. It would be prudent long term management for the bank to start to plan for this capital infusion today, knowing that it will be necessary within the five-year framework. The only other course is to change the growth rate and the profitability efficiency of the bank so that the capital adequacy does not fall below the 7% level. The planning, however, presents the problem to you graphically, and gives you some alternatives with sufficient time to be able to solve the problem without having to impose a crash solution without long term strategic planning alternatives.

Capital adequacy is one of the few areas in commercial banking where the requirements and constraints have changed so many times in recent years that the subject must be covered in generalities. If we gave you conditions necessary to have capital adequacy for 1985, these prescriptions would be of no value for you in 1987, 1989, or 1991. The federal regulatory agencies have changed capital standards three times in 2-1/2 years, and there is no reason to believe that capital standards won't change as many times in the future. Therefore, stay aware of your regulatory agencies guidelines in order to know exactly where you stand in relation to capital standard. One thing is certain,

Figure 6-2   Impact of Asset Growth on Capital Position

	Base	Year 1	Year 2	Year 3	Year 4	Year 5
Average Assets	$10,000.0	$10,700.0	$11,449.0	$12,250.4	$13,108.0	$14,025.5
Earnings*	$60.0	$62.1	$66.4	$71.1	$76.1	$81.4
Dividends	$15.0	$15.5	$16.6	$17.8	$19.0	$20.4
Capital	$725.0	$771.6	$821.4	$874.7	$931.8	$992.8
Capital/Assets	7.25%	7.21%	7.17%	7.14%	7.11%	7.08%

* On Average Assets

however, if you do not have an adequate capital base, life is going to be miserable at your bank. So make sure you are aware of your capital to asset ratio at all times in order to keep it from falling below adequate levels. You can always cut back on the rate of growth, or try to improve earnings, rather than increase your capital base. Capital inadequacy may be the one financial variable that kills you off unless you watch it carefully.

Personnel Requirements

People run banks, banks don't run people. Or at least that's the management viewpoint. One of your most important (if not the most important) assets is your personnel. Personnel requirements can become a major problem at your bank if not planned for over the long run. And they must be constantly updated to make sure that the personnel fit the operational mode of the bank. Directors retire, management and staff retire, and people unfortunately have untimely demises. Your community bank should have a five-year plan for management recruitment, promotion, and retention. Even more importantly, you must have a plan for management succession as management either dies, retires, or moves to another career opportunity. If you are just one-deep in talent, you are one person short in each position.

Even though it may not be very easy to recruit or maintain good personnel, at least you can clearly determine what personnel are needed. It is a much less ambiguous problem than trying to determine how to cut expenses in order to improve earnings. The only real problem for long term strategic planning is the failure of the Board of Directors and management to recognize this as a problem. This is especially true for senior management who seem to hate to have competent individuals in second tier management positions, because they are afraid the Board of Directors might think that these individuals were more competent than themselves. There is a tendency not to have confident backup persons in the financial institution because they are perceived as a threat to the senior management. If you are a member of the Board of Directors of a community bank, don't let this happen. If your senior management is not at least two-deep, then make sure you make it two-deep. There are many things that can happen to your chief executive officer short of his or her retirement—physical or mental incapacity, death, or even simple resignation for another career opportunity—that would put your bank in deep trouble in the short term. Furthermore, if you as a Board of Directors don't believe that the second person in line would make an adequate chief executive officer, change the circumstances so you will have someone behind the CEO who can do the job. Your bank will have a tendency not to operate very efficiently if you lose your senior management. And if you don't have people standing in line to take over the challenges and responsibilities of the job, you are placing your bank at a very definite disadvantage.

One area of management and personnel requirements that should be noted is the recruitment and retention of confident young bankers. This will be even more evident as new products and services are offered by the community banks. It is often said that the community banks suffer from not being able to hire individuals as competent as those found in the big city banks. We do not believe this is the problem. Where the problem arises is that the small town, community oriented banks don't continually educate their banking personnel as well as the big city banks. One of the commitments that you should have for the long term strategic planning of your bank is the continuing education of your staff personnel. The banking schools, general or specific in nature, should be considered not as a fringe benefit but as a part of the job for your management personnel. Your staff and supervisors should also be encouraged to continue their education whether it is at vocational, community, or baccalaureate college level. There should be a quid pro quo. Employees should be expected to give you detailed outlines of what they have learned at the sessions that they have gone to, and should be responsible for having learned something at these sessions, in addition to having a good time. But they should be encouraged to continue to learn and the expense should be one that all parties know will be spent each year in order to improve the technical expertise of the staff.

If your staff hasn't gone to a banking school of some kind in the last five years, your staff is obsolete. That's how quickly the industry has changed. That is also true for a three-year period of time in the future. Thus, make sure that part of your long term strategic planning in the personnel and manpower areas is to concentrate on upscaling the educational abilities and technical expertise of your staff.

External Expansion Opportunities
As part of the long term strategic planning for your bank, you should determine how much growth can take place from internal perspectives. As management of the Board of Directors you have to decide how quickly you can grow based upon the internal conditions within your marketplace. Internal expansion is simply the ability to be able to grow in terms of deposits, loans, assets, capital and earnings from your present offices within the current marketplace that you have served historically. This is in contrast to external expansion which we will discuss.

The reason why you break these two into separate components is to see how closely your objectives for growth and profitability can be satisfied from internal expansion without having to go out to seek merger or acquisition partners in order to be able to achieve your goal. First you determine your profitability and growth goals and then you determine how much growth and performance you can get from your internal operations. If there is a significant gap, there are several alternatives. You can either limit your growth and performance goals to that of the internal operational efficiency of your firm or, you can try to increase your capacity within the marketplace from an internal standpoint. Finally, you may have to go outside and find someone else to join you in order for you to get the size and efficiency necessary to meet the long term goals your board has set forth.

Each market will necessitate and govern different internal expansion opportunities. It is not important that your market grow twice as fast as some other market does internally. It is important that you understand how you will grow and perform within your own marketplace. Currently, the rust belt provides less internal expansion opportunities than the areas in the sun belt. It is more probable that expansion through merger and acquisition will take place among commercial banking organizations in the rust belt areas than in the sun belt. In many areas of the sun belt, the commercial banking organizations can't keep up with potential expansion opportunities within their own banking market. On the other hand, in the rust belt the market in certain areas may be declining absolutely. This means that if one attempts to look at growth and performance variables over a five-year horizon, it may be necessary to develop an external expansion strategic planning program in order to be able to survive.

Internal Expansion Opportunities
It would seem from the discussion above that external expansion opportunities are substitutes for internal expansion opportunities. That is only partially correct. In fact, external expansion opportunities through merger, consolidation, or acquisition may complement internal expansion opportunities through new products and services and branches. It all depends upon the banking structure of your marketplace, and the opportunities available. If you divide your objectives into both internal and external expansion opportunities you can determine whether the opportunities exceed the bank's objectives and goals or fall short. If the internal opportunities are significantly below the planning parameters, then external expansion will be necessary to meet goals and objectives over the five years forecasted. Then it will be up to the senior management and the Board of Directors to find the appropriate commercial banking organizations, or non-banking subsidiary affiliates, that will provide the growth and

performance parameters that will assist in meeting the goals and objectives. As the banking structure becomes more liberal in the several states of the United States, opportunities are more plentiful throughout the areas served by the community bank. In fact, several community banks may have to form together to survive as an independent entity among all the tall trees of branch banking systems and bank holding companies. Regardless of the banking structural parameters of your market, external expansion may be the opportunity for you to meet your goals and objectives, if internal expansion won't permit.

It is not as important for external expansion opportunities to be available in your marketplace as it is for you to recognize that it may take external expansion to be able to reach your objectives. Furthermore, if you have determined how much of your goals and objectives can be reached through internal expansion and through external expansion, you can analyze more carefully expansion opportunities that come up and prioritize them so that you do not achieve external expansion victories that blow you right out of your long term game plan. That's more easily said than done, since the merger/acquisition mania becomes paramount over time. But at least you can try to keep your head while everyone else is merging and/or acquiring willy nilly without much reference to the overall game plan. You can always change your game plan if you think conditions have changed so that your goals and objectives should be modified. But as long as you think they are relevant and are to be ascribed to, you should always analyze your internal and external expansion opportunities in line with your overall goals and objectives from a growth and profitability standpoint.

Non-Bank Subsidiary Affiliates

If your community banking organizations happen to be in either a multi-bank holding company or a one-bank holding company, the long run strategic planning should take into consideration non-banking subsidiary affiliate opportunities. The smaller and more remote the community, the less opportunities available to you in the non-banking area. On the other hand, in communities of less than 5,000, commercial banks in major cities are permitted to operate full line insurance agencies. In addition, because of the small size of your community, there may be opportunities to have a mortgage banking subsidiary or at least a subsidiary. Free enterprise doesn't permit for much competition in this area. A part of your long range strategic planning should be to analyze the opportunities available to you in the non-banking subsidiary affiliate areas. Figure 2-4 indicated the types of non-banking subsidiary affiliates that are available to you as of year-end 1984. There is no guarantee that any of these will fit your own particular situation. Analyze your own market areas carefully and see if any of these opportunities may become attractive financial opportunities for you. This is especially appropriate if you are located along a state border, or if you are located in a state that still has relatively restricted branching laws. Non-banking subsidiary affiliates of bank holding companies can operate anywhere in the world, not just within the subscribed area for branching of the bank. Thus, if you are located on the state line, you can operate a loan production office, consumer finance company, mortgage banking subsidiary, or a leasing subsidiary across the state line even though you couldn't operate a branch deposit-taking facility in the same location. In states where unit banking is still prevalent, such as Texas or Illinois, non-banking subsidiary affiliates can operate throughout the entire state or even beyond the borders even though branches can't operate beyond 5,000 yards from the main office. There are countless opportunities available for the non-banking subsidiary affiliate organizational forms. If one is appropriate for your local market, you should consider it as a part of your long term strategic planning opportunities.

Products and Services
Product and service development is essential as a part of the long term strategic planning for your bank. This product and service development can be categorized into two segments: products and services not currently offered, and those products and services developed over the five-year planning horizon as they become available to your bank and others.

Current products and services that you do not offer, or do not offer under the same conditions as your bank and non-bank competitors should be analyzed and decisions made whether you will offer such products and services. As Figure 7-1 indicates, you should undertake a comparison of service hours and rates within your marketplace to see how competitive you are in relation to the products and services offered by bank and non-bank competitors. From this analysis your strengths and weaknesses in current product and service delivery will be ascertained. You can then make a judgment based upon the expertise of your management, the availability of funds, and the needs of your customers whether to develop such products and services. This is relatively straightfoward. And after such a comparison of services, hours, and rates has been ascertained, your development of products and services can follow quickly and efficiently.

The long term development of products and services is not as easy to comprehend or to bring on-line. You must do marketing research in your bank to assist in the development of such products and services. Don't expect operations and/or lending to develop such products and services. They are much more operational in nature than creative. You should constantly be in touch with what is going on in the industry. Don't be ashamed of stealing and imitating proven products and services offered by your competitors, or by institutions in other parts of the country. Don't be afraid of being first in your market with a particular product or service. The worst that can happen is that it will not be accepted, and you can certainly delete it. New products and services arrive in the marketplace at all times, some survive and some disappear. At the same time, the efficiency and profitability of old products and services that you have offered for a considerable period of time should be analyzed. If they aren't any good, dump them.

The development of new products and services is not easy. Your bank should participate in an organization such as The Bank Marketing Association, The Bank Administration Institute, The American Bankers Association, and others to be on the forefront of the new products and services that will be offered in your industry. Your staff should be constantly reading what is being published concerning new products and services, and your legal counsel should assist you in developing products and services that will be legal or that may become legal in the next several years based upon the powers and responsibilities granted in the commercial banking industry. Change will be paramount in the product and service delivery system offered by your bank over the next five years. In order for you to keep current, you will have to devote considerable time and resources to the product and service development phase of bank management. The changes have taken place so rapidly in the last five to ten years that you can expect three to five new products and services each year, and the deletion of several that have been around for a long time. You just can't continue to operate with the old products and services that you have been able to develop over the past fifty years and consider yourself competitive within the marketplace. It will be necessary for you to keep developing new products and services in order to have an edge. This development of services and products should be a part of your long term strategic planning process. Again, keep in mind that you can delete products and services that don't pan-out, but if you don't offer such products and services you may lose present customers and never gain other customers because of your inability to compete in the marketplace.

Specific Long Term Strategic Planning Policies

Goals and objectives of long term strategic planning have all been general in nature. Some of the general goals and objectives have had specificity written into them, but they have been overall in nature. As a part of the long term strategic planning process it is necessary also to specify certain types of policies, most of which are required today by the regulatory agencies. As we start to discuss these types of specific policies keep in mind that these can change over time as conditions and legal constraints modify the purposes and functions of these specific policies.

Lending Policy

Each commercial bank is different. The banking markets in which you operate are different. Therefore, don't develop lending policies that work for Citicorp but not for you. Several years ago, in examining a small rural bank in Michigan, it became evident that they had taken the easy way out in developing a lending policy which had been insisted upon by the state banking agency. They simply called up their major correspondent, a money center bank, and received a copy of their lending policy. They typed a new front piece on the lending policy, and dropped it into their file as the new lending policy approved by the Board of Directors. To say that this policy was inappropriate would be an understatement. This was a small $25 million commercial bank which had just adopted a 175 page lending policy, inlcuding sections on international lending and major equipment wholesale leasing. In fact, they even forgot to take the name of the major correspondent bank out of the lending policy except on the front page, and therefore the entire policy was replete with the wrong bank's name.

Develop your own lending policy to meet your needs. You should develop comprehensive lending policies for those areas that you are going to utilize as major lending components. Your staff should assist in the development of these lending policies. The Board of Directors should approve the general parameters of the lending policy, and authorize the appropriate delegation of authority to the officers of the bank to operate such policy. The policy should be long enough to cover all of the areas that you lend in. But, it should not be so cumbersome or unworkable as to make it a joke. Your involvement in the development of this lending policy should be in accordance with how you lend. It will work much more efficiently if you develop your own than if you use a correspondent banks' lending policy or one developed for a friend of yours hundreds of miles away.

One last note in this area before we move on. Make sure that your lending policy is flexible enough to take into consideration changes in statute law, regulation, interpretation, and the marketplace. As lending accomodation changes, your lending policy should be reviewed on a regular basis and modified if necessary to meet the current lending needs and demands of your marketplace. If it turns out that you don't have a lending policy for a particular line of credit, develop one. Just don't wing it—develop a long term lending policy that can be modified to meet changing circumstances.

Since we are talking about long term strategic planning, keep in mind that your lending policy should not only take into consideration what types of loans should be made, but also how you are planning to emphasize your lending talents in the long run. If you are currently real estate oriented, and believe that your marketplace is shifting to a commercial orientation, then the long run strategic lending policies should favor commercial lending. If commercial lending is not a primary focus of your bank, you should develop a long term strategy for real estate and/or consumer lending. Know what is available in your marketplace, what is demanded in your marketplace and how your marketplace is going to change over time. This will assist you in developing a long term strategic plan for your lending function which will be in tune with what opportunities the marketplace offers.

Investment Policy

Here again a policy is probably more constrained by law than by how you and your Board of Directors would like to invest your funds. As a national or state bank, regulation and/or statute may dictate precisely how you may invest funds. On the other hand, in many cases, you may wish to restrict your investment policies more tightly than the laws and regulations permit. Long term strategic planning for your investment portfolio enables you to develop the types of securities and their maturities in such a fashion as to assist in the overall profitability objectives and liquidity goals of the bank. Your investment policies should be developed to indicate which grades and ratings of securities you are willing to purchase and hold in your bank portfolio as well as the range of maturities that you feel appropriate to your bank. Investment policies are designed more in terms of money market and capital market constraints than they are by local market conditions. You should have a review function in your investment policy on a much more regular basis than for other policies developed in the long term strategic planning process. Your investment policy may be a general five-year policy, with specific one-year goals and objectives within such policy. Regular quarterly review of such policy is desirable to determine the applicability of your policy to current market conditions. Your investment committeee should probably meet at least monthly, either as a subcommittee of the Board of Directors, or as a management committee. The investment managers should be on top of the markets at all times and call meetings of the investment committee when necessary to modify the investment policy and/or investment holdings of the bank to ensure liquidity and profitability of the investment portfolio.

You would be surprised at the number of banks that still consider the investment portfolio as a residual. They put the money into reserves, use cash in the vault, and then develop their lending policy. Anything that is left over they throw into securities. This problem developed because a lot of financial institutions sense investment management may be more difficult than lending management. The management of the bank may not feel that it has the expertise to handle the investment portfolio properly. They either fiddle around with it, throw it in the federal funds as a last resort, or turn over the investment policy and implementation to a regional brokerage firm and/or investment advisory firm. If you don't have the expertise internally, you may have to use the advisory firm concept. Even if you do, you should make sure that the investment advisory firm is operating under the investment policy established by the bank. And review should be no less regular because it's being handled by an outside firm. If you are relatively small, and cannot afford an investment manager for your own portfolio, it may be economically prudent to use an investment advisory firm. On the other hand, if you have the resources, and you have expertise on your staff, then an internal investment manager may be more economically efficient than using an outside advisory firm. Either way, develop your own policies to be able to handle this area. It is extremely important over the long run to the liquidity and profitability of your bank.

Security
Most commercial banks do have a security policy. This involves what happens in case of robbery, embezzlement, or fraud. Using the guidelines from your regulatory agency, develop a security plan that will be appropriate to the modern problems of the banking industry. Make sure that it is delegated to the proper functioning units of your bank so that it can be carried out at all times. Security is an everyday problem. But the long term importance of the security policy is that it will protect the bank from uninsurable losses in the long run. Also, make sure that you have insurance coverage of the appropriate amount and kind, in order to cover any potential actual losses.

Auditing
Over the past decade, one of the major problems faced by the community bank is the use of the outside audit furnished by a certified public accounting firm. What is the current status of the auditing function in your bank? Is it one individual auditor? Is it a team of auditors, reporting to the chairman of the board? To whom do they report? As a safeguard to the safety and solvency of your

bank, it is extremely important to develop a long term auditing policy. One of the worst policies is to have a single individual responsible for auditing. We cannot emphasize too strongly that a single auditor may be the major source of possible embezzlement or fraud in your bank. Often this is the only individual who can travel throughout the bank making entry changes as he or she goes. The auditor may be the source of your embezzlement or fraud problem rather than the protector against such fraud and/or embezzlement. We know of at least six occasions in the last five years where the auditor was the source of the embezzlement or fraud and was found out through other means. We highly recommend the use of an outside CPA firm, either with a certified outside audit, or used on an irregular surprise basis to act as auditors for the bank when the bank is not able to afford its own team of internal auditors. An auditor must work both with the management and the Board of Directors, but the auditor's responsibility is to the Board of Directors. Then the operational implementation of changes is delegated by the Board of Directors to management.

The auditing function is a vital one, and must be carefully planned and controlled. Through a series of checks and balances, ranging from the regulatory agency examiners, through the internal accounting department, the internal auditing department, and the external auditing function, safety and solvency of the bank can be insured through appropriate review and accountability. This policy is crucial, and cannot be slighted without having dangerous repercussions.

Personnel

The personnel policy has to do with the treatment of the staff and management of the community bank. As the community bank becomes larger, the more need there will be for a full fledged resources person and a complete series of job descriptions, fringe benefit packages, comparable salaries, and absolute attention to all the state and federal wage and hour laws in order to avoid discriminatory treatment. If your institution is large enough, train someone to be a professional personnel officer and allow them and their staff to develop and implement the personnel policies necessary for a smooth running community bank. If your bank is not large enough for internal personnel, use one of the competent national or regional consultants who specialize in assisting the commercial banking industry in developing appropriate compensation and fringe benefit programs in order to maintain a smooth operating bank. These outside individuals can assist you in developing programs that will work in your bank.

There is no way to operate a commercial bank nowadays on a shoestring without job descriptions, salary and benefit packages, meeting state and federal laws, and overall attention to the well-being of your employees. If you do, you may be one of those banks that the unions will attempt to organize, something that is relatively rare in the banking industry. The development of a personnel policy by your Board of Directors with implementation and review by the management is an important long term strategic plan. It assists in the development of the proper staff.

Other Long Term Policies
Other than the policies already mentioned there are countless others, many may be appropriate for your bank but not for somebody else's. Some examples of other types are community reinvestment act policy, banking hours policy, service charge policy, and lending limits policy. You should develop a long term strategic plan for all of the policies you think are important in your shop. Review them at least on a six-month or a yearly basis to make sure that they are still in accordance with what you are attempting to do with such policies. If the policy isn't doing what it's supposed to be doing, scrap it or modify it. But be sure that you have given it the opportunity to be an appropriate policy and review and modify it when necessary.

Competitive Comparisons

Long term strategic planning cannot be done in a vacuum. We have implied that comparisons have to be made with other commercial banking organizations and other non-bank financial intermediaries. We want to reinforce the fact that commercial banks, whether they be community banks or multinational banks are in competition with other bank and non-bank national intermediaries not only in the local marketplace but also throughout the world. Therefore, when you determine long term strategic planning and its effect upon the environs of the community, you must consider comparison of service hours and rates with bank and non-bank competitors. Furthermore, the decline and rise of the various competitors will be important, as well as their service hours and rates. In reality, the totality of the financial intermediary struggle will impact the survival of the community bank in the marketplace. You, as the community banker, must be aware of the impact of these other non-bank financial intermediaries within your local market, for today as well as for the next five to ten-year horizon. Because each local market is different, no generalization can be made as to their impact. But if some of your customers can achieve a higher yield on funds deposited at money market mutual funds, mutual funds, cash management accounts and other non-bank financial products—either within the local market or access quickly through "800" numbers or wire transfers—these firms become very competitive within your marketplace even if they're not physically located there. They will impact your cost of funds. Don't be misled that the other types of funds do not have insurance. None of them have failed in the last five years; in 1984 eighty banks failed.

This is a warning to be competitive not only with commercial banks, savings and loans, and credit unions but with any type of financial business that purports or alleges to offer a financial product or service. They probably do, and some of your customers or potential customers will use that financial alternative. So consider them a competitor, and figure out how you are going to be able to beat them at their own game. Be imaginative. Be realistic as to who your competitors are. Don't belittle these types of competitors because they take good dollars away from your bank.

In developing a long term strategic plan, use your best judgment to assess what competition will exist within your local market over the five to ten-year horizon. Then modify your strategic plans to take into consideration this degree of competition from other commercial banks and non-bank financial intermediaries. In doing so you will make your forecast far more realistic than if you assume that you operate within a vacuum and no one else is a major competitor of yours.

Contingency Planning

It is the Board of Directors' responsibility to determine contingency plans in case goals contemplated by the board and implemented by management do not culminate in the desired result. Such contingency plans should be considered and approved by the board prior to implementation. Then, if events or conditions arise that necessitate the cancellation of a program, or the significant modification of the implementation process, this can be done quickly without having to call the entire board into session. Such contingency planning is important to the board since it makes them aware of all aspects of the contemplated actions, including those that may adversely impact the proposal. By being so aware of such potential adversities, the implementation of such contingency plans would not be a shock to the board, but simply a rational method to counteract or reverse previous decisions.

Summary

Long term strategic planning is necessary for your bank in order to survive. Without knowing where you are going, it is impossible to get there step-by-step. Once you know how you want to go and how you want to get there, the short term strategic planning can set forth specific goals and objectives, implemented by specific techniques and procedures in order to get to your long term goals and objectives. In the next chapter, we will analyze the short term planning process which is based upon a successful long term strategic planning decision-making process. Neither can be successful without the other and the entire planning process cannot be accomplished efficiently without both elements.

Long term strategic planning involves the bank, its staff, its management, its directors, and its shareholders in the development and implementation of a course of action for a foreseeable period of time. Furthermore, with such a course of action known to all parties, modifications can be made as conditions change. But at all times the ultimate goals and objectives of the bank are known. Without a significant amount of long term strategic planning, it would be impossible to steer the bank in a direction consistent with the wishes of all the parties, since all the parties would not know of the common direction of such implementation of the strategic plan. There could be a lot of things left out in the operation of the bank and it will survive in spite of itself. But, long term strategic planning goals and objectives are not to be left out. Without a long term game plan, the bank is doomed to eventually fail.

7

Short Term Budgeting

Short term budgeting is budgeting for a year or less. It's possible to have short term budgets for one month, a quarter, semi-annually, or a year, but if you haven't done any strategic planning, then the shortest budgeting period you should start with is the yearly budget. After experimenting for several years with yearly budgets, you can develop quarterly and semi-annual budgets.

If you feel like it, prepare your budgets on a monthly, quarterly, semi-annual or yearly basis. It will mean more work at the outset, but it will make more sense for you, and you will have a more sophisticated output to deal with when attempting to reconcile your budgets with actual results.

Yearly Goals and Objectives

As a part of a long term strategic plan, you should break your long term goals and objectives into yearly goals and objectives. This permits you to set intermediate goals and objectives in order to reach your long term results. For example, if you've been earning .6% rate of return on average assets, and your five-year strategic planning has indicated that you want to get to a 1.3% rate of return, then it makes sense to pick a goal each year and achieve it on your way from .6% to 1.3%. For example for the first year you might want to go .7% or.75%. The second year you might want to go to a .9%. The third year you'd achieve 1.0% to 1.1% and then to 1.2% and finally to 1.3% in the fifth year.

The first criterion for setting yearly goals and objectives is to set realistic ones. Using the sample above, if you operated a .6% rate of return last year, and this year's budget is for a 1.2%, this may be completely unrealistic based on the composition of your assets and liabilities. On the other hand, a goal .7% to .75% rate of return on assets might be a realistic goal, one that is achievable, and those who participate in the attainment process will be proud of their efforts. It cannot be stressed enough that failure to reach intermediate goals on the way to long term objectives is more debilitating than not having such goals at all. It frustrates the management, hampers the efficiency of the staff, and over-all affects the activities of the Board of Directors, the management, and the staff. And needless to say, it doesn't make the shareholders happy, either.

Some of the short term goals and objectives that should be accounted for each year when strategic planning takes place are examined in the following paragraph.

Profitability. There are two basic measurements of profitability: return on assets and return on equity. Based on recent performance, regulatory restrictions, and objectives set by the Board of Directors, these two measures of profitability should be the first two that are addressed for short term budgeting purposes. As indicated above, the short term annual objectives for return on assets and equity should be achievable, yet they should also be goals that are above previous performance levels, unless economic conditions forecasted for the ensuing year indicate that this year's profitability estimates are as high as could possibly be achieved. If so, then maintaining this year's profitability would be as stimulating a goal as attempting to increase one's profitability under more attractive conditions.

Capital Adequacy. Although capital adequacy is considered a long term strategic planning objective, it can be influenced in the short term by many factors, especially when regulatory agencies are breathing down the backs of community bankers. Therefore, on a yearly basis, profitability and retention of earnings can significantly impact adequacy. In addition, it may be necessary to issue preferred stock or sell subordinated debentures or mandatory debentures in order to meet capital requirements. In most cases, these projects are done within a very short period of time, so this usually occurs within the short term planning framework.

Dividend Policy. This goes hand in hand with capital adequacy. Dividends paid out to shareholders in community banks are usually established over the long term, and range between 20% and 40% of each year's profit. If capital adequacy is inadequate, a decline in the dividend pay-out ratio may be necessitated, or dividends may have to be eliminated completely, in order to conform to regulatory requirements. Dividend policy is not a residual, but is often a very active important and sensitive issue that has to be planned for in the community bank in the short term.

Non-Interest Income. Based upon comparisons with competitors, short term budgeting should include the establishment of charges for service charges, night depository fees, money orders, notaries, trust services, safety deposit boxes, traveler's checks, and other non-interest oriented fees garnered by the community bank. These fees should not be out of line, but at the same time never should be adjusted to make sure that incomes are in line, or even slightly leading the competitors within the marketplace. Dollars of income earned through fees and service charges can become major factors for increased profitability for the organization.

Non-Interest Expenses. Every time we talk about short term budgeting, everybody talks about cutting back on non-interest expenses. Well, this book is no different. In the long term, you can cut down on non-interest expenses, but in the short term it's even much more critical. When one plans ahead for the next year, and one needs to cut back on expense, then one must do so through non-interest expenses initially. They may not save the day, but they certainly will get you through the morning. Therefore, it is extremely important to make sure that your non-interest expenses are cut down as low as possible, while at the same time keeping in mind that you must have at least an adequate staff and other expenses to keep the firm operating efficiently.

Interest Expense. Here's an area that everybody feels really can't be controlled, even under these days of deregulation. It can, and for short term swings, it must be. If you as a commercial banker do not understand a comparison of service hours and rates analysis, then you are not prepared to analyze the competitive rate conditions within your marketplace. Figure 7-1 is a comparison of service hours and rates tables that could be used to analyze comparative rates and services within the marketplace. This type of comparison indicates to the community banker exactly how his or her rates are doing in relation to the competition. If this type of analysis is used, quarter after quarter, bank management can ascertain whether they are on top of or behind competitive conditions within the marketplace. You will note that this comparison of service hours and rates table not only covers interest rates paid on deposits, but also interest rates based on loans, service charges, services rendered, and hours of operation. These indicators can clearly indicate what your competitive posture is, and can be very helpful in your short term planning on a quarterly basis to determine where you are in relation to your competitors. Thus, it can help achieve the yearly objectives that you have set for your institution.

Personnel. Although personnel is handled in aggregate under non-interest expense, attention to personnel costs and personnel requirements is essential to short term budgeting and planning. Total cost of personnel is important. But the composition of such personnel in order to meet the efficiency requirements of the bank is also important. Careful attention to the types of personnel needed and their cost is extremely important in the short term budgeting and planning process.

Asset and Liability Management. As outlined elsewhere in this book, appropriate short term asset and liability management is essential for proper planning. Considerable time has to be spent to ensure the appropriate asset composition for appropriate levels of profitability (rates of return on assets). At the same time, careful attention has to be paid not only to the volume of liabilities, but also their changing composition as new financial instruments bring increased risk and uncertainty to the community bank. Appropriate management of the net interest market (the spread) and the emphasis on appropriate gap management over the short term are absolutely necessary for the survival of the community bank.

Classified Assets

Classified assets and other problems raised by regular bank examinations must be cleared up as quickly as possible. These are not long term strategic planning goals, but are problems that must be erased immediately. Thus, if such problems have occurred, emphasis must be placed in the short term on correcting such problems. Often these problems interact with the others mentioned, but at no time should they be set aside or placed on the back burner when analyzing short term strategic planning goals and objectives.

This list was meant to indicate the types of problems short term planning must strive to solve. At the same time, they project the organized planning mode under which the commercial bank must operate. Short term planning, often called budgeting for short, is often considered to be nothing more than projecting profitability for the upcoming year. There are many other aspects of short term planning that must be analyzed by the community banker in order to make sure the operation runs smoothly. If the emphasis is only on profitability, then other aspects can become unravelled during the year. Thus,

Figure 7-1 Comparison of Pricing and Services

Name of Financial Institution

	Name	Name	Name
Hours: Lobby			
Mon.–Thurs.			
Friday			
Saturday			
Other			
Hours: Drive-In			
Mon.–Thurs.			
Friday			
Saturday			
Other			
Services: (Y/N)			
Safe Deposit			
Night Deposit			
Travelers Checks			
Money Orders			
Bank By Mail			
Phone Transfers			
Utility Bill Collect.			
Sr. Citizen Free Chkg			
Trust Dept./Services			
Community Room			
Credit Cards:			
Master Card			
Visa			
Amex-Gold			

Name of Financial Institution

	Name	Name	Name
Rates & Charges:			
Consumer Cds:			
Maturity/Rate			
Maturity/Rate			
Maturity/Rate			
Maturity/Rate			
Auto Loans–New:			
Maturity/Rate			
Maturity/Rate			
Maturity/Rate			
Auto Loan–Used:			
Maturity/Rate			
Maturity/Rate			
Maturity/Rate			
Home Improve Loans:			
Maturity/Rate			
Maturity/Rate			
Maturity/Rate			
Maturity/Rate			
Mortgage Loans:			
(20 Year Amort.)			
95/5			
90/10			
80/20			
75/25			

Student Loans
IRAs
Keogh Plans
Auto. Teller Machines

Rates & Charges

Personal Checking:
Bal./Elim. Serv. Chg
Monthly Serv. Charge

Business Checking:
Monthly Serv. Chg
Per Check Chg
Deposit Chg
Earnings Credit

Other Checking/Now:
Monthly Serv. Chg
Minimum Balance
Highest Rate Paid
Minimum Rate Paid

Mortgage Loans:
(30 Year Amort.)
95/5
90/10
80/20
75/25

Real Estate Loans:
Farm (Term/Secured)

Commercial (Term/secured)
1 Yr Working Cap.
5 Yr Fixed Asset

Signature Loans:
Unsecured 1 Yr, $1000

Credit Cards:
Interest on Unpaid Bal.
Annual Fee

the profitability objectives cannot be reached. We are not suggesting that profitability objectives are not important, but profitability should not be the exclusive objective of any community bank. Once historical data have been analyzed, short term planning depends on establishing budgets and adhering to them. Or, at least reasons or rationalizations should be made as to why the budgets are no longer applicable.

Budgets assist management in determining exactly what actions to follow over the short run, whether it be in the auditing department, the branch administration area, or the general administrative expense area. They permit an institution to divide itself into profit centers and cost centers, because they do exist, and attempt to achieve the interim goals and objectives set forth by senior management and the Board of Directors. Budgets are simply scientific estimates of the potential income and expenses for the short run. They are established to guide and to control future income and expense in order to achieve the short term goals and objectives set forth.

Needless to say, variances from budgets do occur over the short run. These variances are volume variances (i.e., the variances occur because the incomes or costs are greater than were anticipated at the beginning of the budgetary period); rate variances (i.e., variances to the income and expense categories of the financial institutions created by extraneous rate forces not foreseen in the budgetary process) or mix variances.

Mix variances result from a change in the composition of the business done by the financial institution, even though the general costs were in line, assuming that the mix had not changed. For example, if savings accounts were expected to remain stable during the year, and declined by 25%, this would be a mix variance. Overall, since the total volume of business had not increased, this would not have been a volume difference. And, since the rates were relatively close to the estimates by managements, it would not be a rate variance. Thus, any deviations from the budget as outlined by management and approved by the board of directors at the beginning of the period resulted from changing composition, subject to less control than volume variances, but about as elusive as rate variances.

Since the budgets are used not only to establish short term goals and objectives but also to control the expenses of the financial institution, their follow-up and review are essential. Budgets that are established initially and never reviewed, modified, or scrapped completely are useless to the financial institution. In essence, a short term goal or objective as reflected by a financial budget for the year 1985 may be broken into quarterly or even monthly budgets; as each month or quarter goes by, the remainder of the year's budget may be modified to reflect what is going on in 1985, rather than simply to retain the same budget the entire year, and comment at board meetings on variance statistics.

The review, and consequent modification if necessary, to the budget process established by the senior management of the financial institution is relevant to the senior management only if they use the budget for purposes of control and review of the income and expense of the institution. If goals and objectives are to be achieved, they must be achieved in the real world, which is the marketplace of competition, and not simply in an abstract budget. The budget is simply a tool for measuring such goals and objectives. Therefore, it is important for the financial institution management to review and modify such budgets in the short run, especially if they are not on target with the goals and objectives.

Finally, the goals and objectives must also be changed if economic and financial conditions will not permit the goals and objectives to be achieved. If the goals and objectives are not being achieved, not because of economic and financial conditions beyond the control of the financial institution but because of managerial inefficiencies, and/or incompetencies, then it is up to the Board of Directors of the institution to take remedial steps to improve the management.

As examples of quantifying short range goals and objectives, budgets permit the board of directors to assess the performance of its senior management in achieving such goals and objectives. Obviously, these are not the only gauges of financial performance for the senior management. But if such goals are specific and attainable, and are not attained by the senior management, it must be assumed that senior management is incapable of operating the financial institution in a competent manner. Thus, the attainment or lack of attainment of budgetary goals and objectives in the short run, as well as over the long run, indicates to the Board of Directors the degree of competence of its management. In this same context, if management is able to make significant strides in reversing disastrous results, or in achieving the positive gains set forth in the previous period, then corporate management should be judged as competent, and the goals and achievements set rationally for the next period.

There is a burden upon the Board of Directors of financial institutions not to set unobtainable goals and objectives and then discipline or replace the management for the inability to meet such outrageously inaccessible goals. This has happened in the past, and is sure to happen again in the future. On the other hand, it is a basic affront to the management of a financial institution to have this type of budgetary goal-setting evolve in the short run.

Budgeting

The significance of yearly budgeting cannot be overstated. In line with the long terms goals for profitability as discussed in Chapter 6, it is necessary to plan carefully and in great detail the yearly approaches to the goals and objectives. Although the Board of Directors and senior management may determine that the goals and objectives can be significantly different over a 3-5 year horizon, each yearly budget is derived from historical performance, especially last year's. The yearly budget considers modifications for changes that have either taken place in the national economy or forecasted to do so, coupled with changes in local economy, interest rates, and other factors that will impact upon the operational performance of the bank. The long term profitability goals may be vastly different from last year's performance, but in order to get there, small yearly changes in the budgeting performance must take place.

If you haven't budgeted, this section will be valuable. If you have, this section may be of interest because certain techniques or budgeting aspects outlined may not be those that you have used in the past. It is extremely important to realize that first attempts of budgeting will be crude approximations of the result. However, as you learn from your experience, your technique for budgeting will be greatly improved over time, and if you carefully analyze the actual results in relation to the projected performance, you will gain from your variances not only experience, but also the realization of how expense and income performances differ greatly over short periods of time.

Even though we noted earlier that budgeting should be done on a yearly, semi-annual, quarterly, or monthly basis, we recommend that the budgeting be done on a monthly basis over a yearly framework. This permits for the best overall analysis of the performance of your bank. It permits the best historical record of achievements year-to-date as well as monthly over a several year planning horizon. Furthermore, since most commercial banks in the United States are on the accrual system, accrued income and expense items will be more clearly reflected on month to month changes than they would have been on a cash basis. If your bank is on a cash basis, your budget planning will have to take into consideration the irregular and non-periodic inflows of income in relation to the more regular expense outflows of your bank. Therefore, if you are still on a cash counting system, this budgeting process will be of less material value to you than if you have been forced over to the accrual system because of your size.

One other caveat before we turn to the specific budgeting process. This has to do with the multitude of scenarios that should be run on your behalf while doing budgeting. There is no one perfect budgeting forecast for your bank over the next fiscal year. You and your Board of Directors will decide on a budget, based either on historical performance or best business judgment. That will be what you attempt to achieve over the next fiscal planning period. However, it will be a consensus of many different budgeting scenarios, especially on the income side, and may actually be a compromise between factions of the management and/or the Board of Directors. In 1983, one local financial institution developed twelve different budgeting scenarios, all the way from bankruptcy to a 2% rate of return on assets. You develop such scenarios because you have to take into consideration all of the possible, not just probable, variations that can take place based upon uncertain economic and financial conditions faced by your bank. We do not recommend the development of twelve scenarios, but we do recommend the development of at least three. The three scenarios that we would develop are worst case, probable case, and best possible case scenarios based upon future forecasts of interest rates, both on the asset and liability sides of the balance sheet, and based upon other conditions that impact income and expense flows.

You should know that the first step in short term budgeting is to determine income flows for the fiscal year. They should be done on a monthly basis, culminating in a yearly income aggregate. These income statistics should be broken down for each specific income item within the bank's environment. No type of income should be ignored, and changes in charges for service charges, night depositories, etc. should be taken into consideration in budgeting for the year. Monthly changes in income should be forecasted, especially as volumes of loans and investments differ over the year. Also, positional changes in the income stream should be noted to reflect the difference between security and loan volumes as demand and supply conditions change over the year faced by the bank.

Forecasting expenses for the year always seems easier than determining income flows. Except for interest sensitive expenses, such as interest on deposits and non-deposit liabilities, the non-interest-sensitive expenses can be easily forecasted, even if they can't be controlled under forecast conditions. As outlined in the following presentation, expenses can be ascertained with a great deal of specificity, except for interest expenses. So, variations from budgets should be less in these areas than in any other portion of the forecast.

Interest expenses can be forecasted in line with projected deposit and liability flows, based on historical experience, and on forecasts of the national and local economy for the forthcoming fiscal year. Interest expenses are not only affected by the volumes of deposit and liabilities sources of funds anticipated, but are also a reflection of the compositional change in the aggregate funds base. The interest expense, like the income flows, will be the greatest source of variation between projected budgets and actual experience, and thus must be closely monitored to keep the budget within perspective on a monthly basis.

It should be noted that the short-term budgets discussed are more achievable today through the use of the microcomputer. Whereas, in the past, planners have been able to develop only 3-5 scenarios using the hand calculator, it is now possible through the use of any microcomputer to develop 10-15 scenarios. Since many items of the budget are relatively fixed, such as salaries, overhead costs, computerization costs, it is relatively simple to change the assumptions concerning the cost of funds, the rate of return on investments, and the rate of return on loans in order to be able to develop a large number of scenarios. Microcomputer costs are far less than one salaried individual's cost, are depreciable, and they don't retire, take vacations, or leave for other commercial banks. The microcomputer will become your best asset in forming the short-term budgeting scenarios necessary for your management and board of directors to determine the appropriate fiscal budgets for the next planning period.

Let us assume some basic variable parameters to analyze the budgeting process in the commercial bank. Keep in mind that all of the expenses will be kept constant, except for interest expense, even though in reality you may wish to vary your non-interest expenses along with the interest income and interest expense categories as the budgetary year progresses.

The following assumptions for the initial budgeting process have been determined:

1. Rate of return on commercial loans is 11.0%
2. Rate of return on installment loans is 15.0%
3. Rate of return on mortgage loans is 13.0%
4. Service charges are estimated to be 0.50% of average assets
5. Other miscellaneous income is estimated to be 0.50% of average assets
6. Interest expense is estimated to be:
   a. Passbook and statement savings accounts — 5.5%
   b. Certificates of deposit — 9.0%
   c. Money market deposit account — 8.0%
7. Rate of return on securities:
   a. Government securities — 9.5%
   b. Federal agency securities — 10.0%
   c. Municipal securities — 7.5%
   d. Federal funds — 9.0%

Figure 7-2(a)   ABC Bank Average Balance Sheet

Assets	($ Millions)	Rate of Return (%)
Cash & Due	$ 5.0	0.00
Securities:		
U.S. Treasury	10.0	9.50
Agencies	10.0	10.00
Municipal	5.0	7.50
Federal Funds	3.0	9.00
Loans:		
Commercial	20.0	11.00
Installment	20.0	15.00
Mortgage	20.0	13.00
Other Real Estate Owned	1.0	0.00
Premises & Equipment	4.0	0.00
Other Assets	2.0	0.00
Total Assets	$100.0	

Liabilities & Equity	($ Millions)	Interest Expense (%)
Deposits:		
Demand Deposits	$ 10.0	0.00
Savings	20.0	5.50
Money Market	10.0	8.00
Time Deposits (CDs)	50.0	9.00
Other Borrowed $	0.0	0.00
Other Liabilities	2.0	0.00
Total Liabilities	$ 92.0	
Equity	8.0	
Total Liabilities & Equity	$100.0	

Assuming the variables listed on page 98, Figure 7-2 indicates the budgeting parameters for the ABC Bank for the year 198X. Note that these statistics are not necessarily consistent throughout, taking into consideration certain flows over time.

Now let us change the assumptions as follows for the next budgeting process.

Figure 7-2(b)   ABC Bank State of Income—1

Income	($ Millions)	
Interest on Loans:		
Commercial	$2.200	
Installment	3.000	
Mortgage	2.600	
Total		$ 7.800
Interest on Securities:		
Government	$0.950	
Agencies	1.000	
Municipals	0.375	
Federal Funds	0.270	
Total		$ 2.595
Total Interest Income		$10.395

Expenses		
Interest on Deposits:		
Savings	$1.100	
Money Market	0.800	
Time Deposits (CDs)	4.500	
Total Interest Expense		$ 6.400
Net Interest Income		$ 3.995
Other Income:		
Service Charge		0.500
Other		0.500
Total Expenses		$ 4.000
Income Before Taxes		$ 0.995

1. Rate of return on commercial loans — 14.0%
2. Rate of return on mortgage loans — 11.0%
3. Rate of return on installment loans — 17.0%
4. Cost of funds:
   a. Passbook savings and statement savings — 5.5%
   b. Certificates of deposit — 10.0%
   c. Money market deposits — 11.0%
5. All other variables stay the same
6. Rate of return on securities:

a. Rate of return on government — 10.0%
b. Rate of return on federal agencies — 10.5%
c. Rate of return on municipal (pre tax) — 8.0%

Figure 7-3 indicates how the budgeting process has changed over time. We have kept the projected volumes of deposits the same, but have simply

Figure 7-3   ABC Bank Statement of Income—2

Income		($ Millions)
Interest on Loans:		
Commercial	$2.800	
Installment	3.400	
Mortgage	2.200	
Total:		$ 8.400
Interest on Securities:		
Government	$1.000	
Agencies	1.050	
Municipals	0.400	
Federal Funds	0.240	
Total:		$ 2.690
Total Interest Income		$11.090
Expenses		
Interest on Deposits:		
Savings	$1.100	
Money Market	1.100	
Time Deposits (CDs)	5.000	
Total Interest Expense		$ 7.200
Net Interest Income		$ 3.890
Other Income:		
Service Charge		.500
Other		.500
Total Other Income:		1.000
Total Income:		$ 4.890
Total Expenses:		4.000
Income Before Taxes		$ .890

changed the rates to access the impact of rates on the overall budgeting process.

In this regard, we shall keep the rates as they were in the budgeting process under Figure 7-2 but shall change the volumes to reflect an increase of 10% for each category over what they were in the original projections. This will not change the rates of return, but simply the volume of income, as well as the volume of expense. Thus, as reflected in Figure 7-4 the budget forecast changes the profit under Figure 7-2 from $995,000 dollars to $1,395,000 dollars under the Figure 7-4 scenario. We haven't changed the rates, simply the volume.

Figure 7-4   ABC Bank Statement of Income—3

Income	($ Millions)	
Interest on Loans:		
Commercial	$2.420	
Installment	3.300	
Mortgage	2.860	
Total		$ 8.580
Interest on Securities:		
Government	$1.045	
Agencies	1.100	
Municipals	0.413	
Federal Funds	0.297	
Total		$ 2.855
Total Interest Income		$11.435
Expenses		
Interest on Deposits:		
Savings	$1.210	
Money Market	0.880	
Time Deposits (CDs)	4.950	
Total Interest Expense		$ 7.040
Net Interest Income		$ 4.395
Other Income:		
Service Charge		0.500
Other		0.500
Total Expenses		$ 4.000
Income Before Taxes		$ 1.395

Figure 7-5   ABC Bank Statement of Income—4

Income	($ Millions)	
Interest on Loans:		
Commercial	$2.420	
Installment	3.300	
Mortgage	2.080	
Total		$ 7.800
Interest on Securities:		
Government	$0.950	
Agencies	1.000	
Municipals	0.375	
Federal Funds	0.270	
Total		$ 2.595
Total Interest Income		$10.395
Expenses		
Interest on Deposits:		
Savings	$1.045	
Money Market	1.080	
Time Deposits (CDs)	4.275	
Total Interest Expense		$ 6.400
Net Interest Income		$ 3.995
Other Income:		
Service Charge		0.500
Other		0.500
Total Expenses		$ 4.000
Income Before Taxes		$ 0.995

Finally, Figure 7-5 changes the composition of deposits and the assets even though it does not change the total volume as projected for the bank's activity. In Figure 7-5, we are changing the mix of the assets and the liabilities to reflect the following:

1. Commercial loans — increase 10%
2. Mortgage loans — decrease 20%
3. Installment loans — increase 10%
4. Checking accounts — stay the same
5. Passbook savings account — decrease 5%

6. Certificates of deposits — decrease 5%
7. Money market deposits — increase 35%

These changes in Figure 7-5 indicate that a compositional change of the projections will have an impact upon the overall performance of the bank. Thus, we have changed the projections in three ways from the initial projections, noting changes in rates, volumes of activity, and also the composition of the assets and liabilities at the same volume level. All of these can be anticipated, and under realistic conditions, all will take place simultaneously. It is up to you as a commercial banker to tie together all of the projected volume, rate, and mix changes so that your forecast is realistic within your own marketplace.

It should be noted also that the rates have been kept the same for the entire period of time. Under realistic conditions these rates will not stay the same. You must estimate how the rates may change over the year, and plug in rate changes both on rates of return on assets and on funds costs in those months. After that you can anticipate changes in the pricing of such assets and liabilities. Keep in mind as noted earlier that you also must pay attention to non-interest expenses that will change as you add or delete personnel, find increased occupancy cost (through additional heating or air conditioning for example) or run across other non-interest expenses unanticipated at the time of budgeting.

These budgets, illustrative as they are, are far more sophisticated than even half of the banks in the United States have prepared at the present time. The more sophisticated you are preparing short-term budgets for your institution, the more you'll be able to react efficiently and correctly when conditions change that will affect your ability to perform in light of the goals and objectives set by your bank.

Asset and Liability Management

Asset and liability management is a funds management approach which has gained in popularity during the latter part of the 1970s and the early part of the 1980s. It should be noted, however, that this approach is not a new managerial concept, but a much more sophisticated adaptation of selected managerial systems previously emphasized. There have been several steps in the development of asset and liability management.

During the 1950s, a managerial concept described as "asset allocation" was emphasized. This was a period characterized by an abundance of relatively stable, low-cost funds, extremely conservative investment planning, and vast amounts of continuous liquidity. Spreads were achieved on various investments and maintained to their maturity. No severe pressure existed for depository financial institutions to improve profitability above and beyond existing levels. Competition as we know it today was relatively nonexistent.

During the decade of the 1960s, a shift away from asset allocation toward "liability management" occurred. A tremendous rate of economic growth took place during this decade as a result of technological innovations which gave rise to an extraordinary increase in the demand for funds. This phenomenon caused interest rates to increase significantly. Also, during the 1960s, demand deposits dominated the liability structure of commercial banks, comprising approximately 64% of total funds. Although a greater proportion of deposits has shifted into passbook savings accounts, a majority of this decade was characterized by abundant, relatively inexpensive sources of funds. Adequate spreads between the cost of funds and corresponding yields were consistently maintained throughout the assets' maturation, and profitability continued to increase.

During the decade of the 1970s, emphasis shifted away from the balance sheet, to income statement management, coined as "profitability management." The period of "tight money" which occurred in the latter part of the 1960s and the early part of the 1970s exerted earnings and liquidity pressures not previously experienced by depository institutions. Interest rates rose continuously, forcing financial institutions to place heavy emphasis on liability management. The amount of inherent risk in all asset categories increased, while the funds for these assets continued to become more expensive. Interest rates during the 1973-75 period reached double digits for the first time since the Depression. Overextensions resulted in record numbers of foreclosures and bankruptcies. For the remainder of the 1970s, management concentrated primarily on improving the bottom line. Deposit compositions began to shift out of the inexpensive demand-deposit categories, which now comprised only 40% of the total commercial bank funds (a decrease of 24%), while interest rate volatility continued. As the cost of funds to finance fixed-rate loans and investments increased significantly, interest margins were reduced more frequently and more substantially. As a result of the high inflation and extreme interest-rate volatility during the early 1980s, it has become quite evident that profitability can only be achieved by implementing coincident asset and liability management plans. Consequently the managerial concept that has now evolved is referred to as asset and liability management. Historically, business cycles have caused fluctuations in interest rates which affect the volume and mix of the financial institution's asset and liability portfolio.

Asset and Liability Management: An Integrated Funds Management Policy

Recently, asset and liability management as a funds management concept has been confused with the idea of money management. The latter refers to the task of converting liquid assets into cash as current needs dictate. Asset and liability management, however, is an integrated funds management approach which examines the financial institution's total balance sheet regularly over time. Such factors as rates, maturities, capital gains and losses, and inclusive and exclusive levels of risk are all factors that must be incorporated into decisions that attempt to improve profitability over time, either by increasing yields on investments or by minimizing the cost of funds utilized. Generally speaking, interest rates on assets and liabilities move together. In a rising rate environment, the amount earned on a floating rate asset increases while the cost of floating liabilities increases, producing little or no effect on net profitability resulting from interest rate changes. Earnings can be improved only to the degree that interest-sensitive assets and interest-sensitive liabilities can be mismatched. Therefore, it is imperative for management to estimate the volume of liquidity needed over time for those unexpected, irregular excess demands for or supply of funds.

Interest Rates and Business Trends

In general, any financial institution's liquidity position is affected by general economic conditions as well as by national, regional, and local business conditions. At one extreme of basic trends that influence the economy, we have secular trends, which are the long term consistently developing trends over time. At the other extreme we have intermediate cycles which are short term and volatile in nature. For an analysis of liquidity, management need not be concerned with the long term secular trends, since they have little impact upon a financial institution's liquidity position. However, the cycles or the interim volatile conditions do require the attention of management in structuring the liquidity policy to effectively cope with ramifications resulting from the periodic supply of and demand for funds.

Factors Affecting Liquidity

The volume of liquidity to be maintained for the volume of funds accessible to a financial institution depends on various internal and external factors. Management has little or no control over many of those factors—the internal growth and composition of deposits, the growth and composition of loans, and the level of purchased funds. In terms of deposits, the rates paid on deposit instruments and the degree to which certain types of deposits are advertised have some bearing on the growth and composition of the deposit portfolio. Likewise, the philosophy and the desire of management to make loans are controlled by management. It should be noted, however, that these internal variables are not totally controllable, since they are significantly impacted by external variables.

External variables over which management has little or no control are the level of interest rates; the rate of inflation; the level of local, regional or national competition; and the present economic conditions and prospects for economic growth. Such external variables might not preclude a financial institution from generating liquidity through liabilities; however, it may have a bearing on the specific liability instruments utilized to provide such liquidity. For example, if within a financial institution's local market area, competition is keen for short term certificates of deposit funds, an institution may find itself purchasing liquidity in the federal funds market.

Figure 7-6 examines asset and liability liquidity characteristics for various segments of an interest rate/business cycle. In the first segment, interest rates reach the low for a particular cycle, signifying a very depressed business economy where demands for funds are at a minimum.

As money becomes very inexpensive, it becomes worthwhile once again for a business to leverage itself. The second cycle reveals economic expansion. During this phase of the business cycle, demand for products increases, and as a result, inventory levels and production increase. The increased demand for funds places pressure on supply, and interest rates begin to rise. In the third stage of high interest rates, inventory levels are at their peaks, production reaches its peak, cuts are made, and the demand for funds is curtailed. As the demand for funds declines, interest rates decline. We then reenter the first stage of the second cycle where demands for funds reach an all-time low, and consequently interest rates reach the lower limits of the cycle, until the point in time where inventories have been totally expanded.

It is not imperative that specific interest rates be predicted for the liquidity purposes of asset and liability management. It is important to estimate the supply and demand for funds in each segment of the interest rate/business cycle in order to attempt to establish a plan of action for various scenarios which could result from potential cyclical activities. By so doing, a particular institution can determine how best to derive the liquidity it needs. Figure 7-6

Figure 7-6   Asset and Liability Liquidity Characteristics for Various Segments of the Interest Cycle

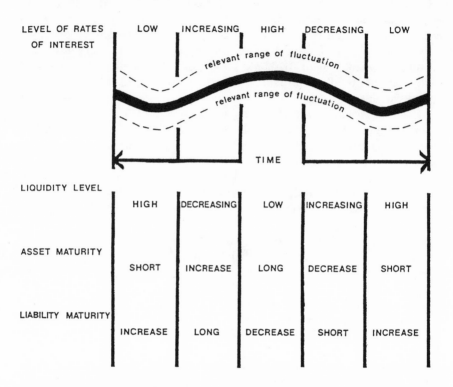

also reveals general liqudity levels through the interest cycle as well as optimum asset and liability maturities which would be in force during each segment. Through the initial segment of lower interest rates, the lack of demand for loans as well as the low rates of interest available on investments results in a high liquidity position, which decreases as the demand for loans increases in the second segment of the cycle. As interest rates peak, when the demand for loans reaches peak levels, an institution's liquidity will be at a minimum. As shown in Figure 7-6, asset maturities are at their shortest in those segments where interest rates are lowest, while it behooves management to lock into longer asset maturities when interest rates reach their peak. Liability maturities should be lengthened when interest rates are low and obviously should decrease when interest rates reach their peak.

This maturity philosophy would maximize profits if in fact it could be achieved. However, it is imperative that financial institutions examine the present composition of their asset and liability portfolio, since most institutions are not totally flexible and cannot significantly change the maturity structure of their portfolio to conform to the profit maximizing strategy of Figure 7-6.

Forms of Liquidity

Liquidity can take the form of asset liquidity or liability liquidity. Asset liquidity is derived by allowing short-term assets to run off or to be sold, while liability liquidity refers to the ability to raise funds via the acquisition of deposits or other borrowed funds. Whether liquidity is best managed by maintaining a reserve of assets that can be readily converted into cash, or by securing deposits or borrowed funds (or historically having the ability to secure or borrow funds) has been an item of perennial contention.

Management of financial institutions today must look to both sources under any set of circumstances to determine the optimal approach for a specific institution at a particular time. Generally speaking, liquidity will be generated from the least expensive source while it should be stored in the highest-yielding alternative available, tempered to a degree by maturity or timing considerations. Therefore, at times liquidity will be less costly if assets are sold, and on other occasions it will be less costly to issue liability instruments.

Liquidity Planning
Management must determine need and then develop a plan for achieving the desired amount of liquidity and acceptable alternatives for generating that volume. It is also important to establish contingency plans in case additional liquidity should be required or excess liquidity must be invested. With respect to commercial banks, data revealed, ". . . that the level of bank capital has not been materially related to bank failures. Rather, bank failures have been principally caused by illiquidity."[1]

It is therefore imperative for management to segregate those assets that are liquid from those that are not and determine which liability sources are available for liquidity purposes. It must also differentiate between those liability items that are stable (core deposits) and those that are volatile (hot money/purchased funds).

Asset Liquidity
Assets that are to be included within the liquidity account should only be those that can be converted to cash quickly and without risk of loss. They must be of

significantly high quality to be readily marketable without having to take a discount on the sale. They need not generate an extremely high rate of return.

Within the liquid asset portfolio, there should be diversification of the types of assets held along with a scheduling of maturities from 1 to 90 days or so. These assets must be traded actively on a daily basis, and must be readily identifiable securities such as Treasury Bills, Federal Funds, loans under agreement to repurchase, bankers' acceptances, and commercial paper. Often, due to timing, the sale of an asset for liquidity purposes may result in a capital loss.

Liability Liquidity

Liability management has similarly provided some significant benefits to those institutions that have historically utilized asset management. Liabilities to be considered as effective potential sources of liquidity should be those that can be acquired quickly, permit flexibility in repayment, and are inexpensive to administer above and beyond the cost of funds. Sources include commercial paper Eurodollars, negotiable certificates of deposit, Federal Funds, and Federal Reserve borrowings. It should be noted that the ability to acquire short-term funds does not protect an institution from incurring possible losses. Short-term funds purchased must be rolled-over frequently, and in fact, when interest rates rise rapidly (as they did during 1979-1981), significant expenses can be incurred which might adversely affect profitability.

Whichever approach is chosen to provide liquidity in a specific situation, alternative sources should be sufficient to cover any unexpected decline in deposits or increased demands for funds. Both current liquidity needs and potential unexpected needs must be combined before an adequate liquidity portfolio can be developed.

The management of each individual institution must evaluate deposit volatility, potential credit demand, investment and loan maturities, and overall investor confidence in the institution prior to being able to adequately determine that institution's liquidity needs.

Individual Institution Analysis

There are several analytical tools that may assist the financial manager to evaluate the present liquidity relationships and liquidity requirements of an institution. The first is a comparative analysis of liquid assets to volatile funds. This analysis is significant in that it establishes for an institution a relationship

based upon historical performance of those assets available for liquidity purposes relative to the potential need for liquidity resulting from volatile liabilities. Figure 7-7 is a sample balance sheet for a financial institution with
summaries of the liquid and nonliquid components of the average daily asset
balance and the proportions of its liability and capital portfolio which were
classified as either volatile or stable.

As can be seen from Figure 7-7, this institution has an average daily balance for total assets of $159,743,000. Of this total, $21,356,000 or 13.4% is considered to be liquid within a three-month period of time. Consequently,
$138,386,000 or 86.6% of its total asset portfolio is considered nonliquid. Of its
total liability and equity capital position $141,448,000 or 88.5% is regarded as
stable, or that portion which is considered to be the core of liability and capi-

Figure 7-7   Liquidity Summary

| Assets | ($000) Av. Daily Balance $ Amt | 3-Month Period | | | |
| | | Liquid | | Non-Liquid | |
		$ Amt	%	$ Amt	%
Total Cash	9,219	691	7.5	8,528	92.5
Total Investments	44,282	15,499	35.0	28,783	65.0
Total Loans	86,335	2,590	3.0	83,745	97.0
Total Other Assets	19,907	2,576	12.9	17,330	87.1
Total Assets	159,743	21,356	13.4	138,386	86.6

| Liabilities & Capital | Av. Daily Balance $ Amt | Stable* | | Volatile | |
		$ Amt	%	$ Amt	%
Total Deposits	137,792	123,009	89.3	14,783	10.7
Total Borrowed Funds	13,597	10,685	71.6	2,912	21.4
Total Other Liabilities	1,632	1,469	90.0	163	10.0
Total Equity Capital	6,722	6,285	93.5	437	6.5
Total Liabilities & Equity Capital	159,743	141,448	88.5	18,295	11.5

Total Liquid Assets	$21,356	
Total Volatile Funds	18,295	
Excess (Deficit) Liquidity	$ 3,061	

* Core Portion

tal position. Finally, $18,295,000 or 11.5% of its liability and capital position is considered volatile, having a high probability of fluctuation. If one subtracts the total volatile funds from the total liquid asset position, the excess or deficiency in liquidity can be determined. In this case, liquid assets total $21,356,000. Volatile funds total $18,295,000. Therefore, this institution has an excess liquidity position of $3,061,000. This amount must be examined in light of interest rate conditions, and the availability of funds.

Ratios are used by financial institutions to assist them in analyzing their liquidity positions. These include the following:

1. Cash and due plus U.S. Government Securities, plus Federal Funds sold, plus securities purchased under agreement to resell, minus Federal Funds purchased, minus securities sold under agreement to repurchase, divided by total deposits.
2. Loans to deposits.
3. Cash assets minus required reserves plus total U.S. Government Securities, divided by total deposits.

By incorporating the data from Figure 7-7, the following conclusions can be drawn:

Historically, the greatest demand for liquidity has occurred when periods of tight money existed, such as 1966-1969, 1973-1975, and 1979-1981. It should be noted, however, that during these periods all financial institutions required increases in their liquidity position, which significantly affected the cost of both asset and liability sources of liquidity. It is imperative that institutions become aware of their present liquidity position and capabilities, and plan accordingly. Excessive liquidity does not maximize profits, nor does insufficient liquidity, which results in an institution's incurring significant costs in acquiring liability sources of liquidity or experiencing losses in asset liquidation.

Various theories have been developed concerning the frequency with which an institution utilizes asset liquidity or liability liquidity. However, we feel that one cannot generalize until an extensive examination of the institution's balance sheet has been completed and the core versus volatile composition of an institution's portfolio has been determined. This information must be examined in relation to economic conditions, the competitive environment, interest rates, inflation, regulatory requirements and local market conditions. Assets included in a liquidity portfolio should be used for liquidity purposes therefore; maximizing profitability should not be the primary factor affecting a decision whether to incorporate assets in a portfolio for liquidity purposes. By properly planning and evaulating the institution's circumstances, management at times may be able to secure liabilities and invest in short term assets even if interest rate spreads are not adequate at the time the liabilities are secured, if in fact management feels that interest rates will increase significantly in the future, and liquidity needs will increase accordingly.

Techniques of Asset and Liability Management

In recent years, financial institution managers have consistently increased their reliance on interest sensitive, short term purchased funds, such as large denomination certificates of deposit, money-market certificates, Federal Funds, and retail repurchase agreements as sources of funds for lending and investment. Basically, the revenues generated from this type of lending and investment, sometimes referred to as "fund brokering," arise from the spread between interest paid on the short term, interest sensitive funds and the interest revenues received on such loans and investments.

Over the past several years, there has been a tremendous increase in the volatility of short-term interest rates. From 1934 to 1980, there were over 200 fluctuations in prime rate, of which 182 took place between 1970 and 1980 (see Figure 7-8). During the entire decade of the 1970s, the prime rate varied approximately 18 times per year, while during 1980 alone, it changed 42 times!

Not only has the frequency of short term interest rate volatility increased, but the magnitude of these short term changes has also increased. Consequently, acquisition of short term funds to invest in long term assets and investments has resulted in an extremely high variability of the earnings position of depository financial institutions. As a result, emphasis has been placed upon both asset and liability management, and spread management to aid in the difficult task of improving earnings.

Management must incorporate asset and liability management as an integrated management tool by segmenting the asset and liability composition of the institution. Effective management of an institution's portfolio, especially in periods of interest rate volatility, requires a thorough analysis and understanding of interest rate sensitivity, maturity matching (GAP analysis), and knowledge of trends in interest rate yields and spreads.

In addition, economic and political factors, as well as the actions of the DIDC (phasing out of regulation Q) will continue to have an effect on the level as well as the volatility of interest rates in the future. Maintaining adequate margins will require a conscious effort in managing asset and liability portfolios.

Figure 7-8   Prime Rate 1965–1980

Shows yearly range and number of times rate
changed during the course of the year

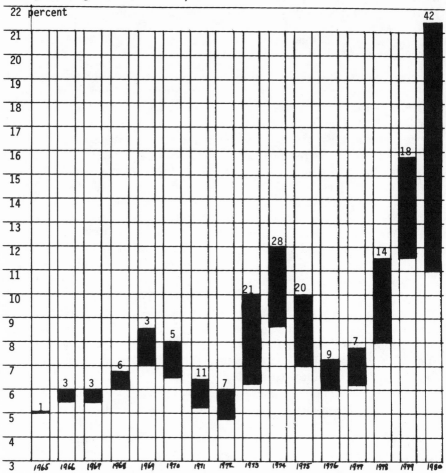

Source: First National Bank of Chicago

Asset and Liability Management as an Integrated Financial Management Policy

It has been proven that the level of interest rates per se has not been the problem in recent years. The problem has been the volatility of interest rates, which has caused tremendous difficulties.

Given either an increasing or a decreasing trend in interest rates, earnings will remain essentially the same if floating rate assets are funded by floating rate liabilities. A study on management of bank interest margins for net interest margins during the rising interest rate period of 1972-1974 and during the falling interest rate period of 1975-1976 concluded that ". . . the 13.2% rise in net interest margin as the cycle peaked in 1974 was virtually matched by the 12.6% rise as the cycle bottomed out in 1976." [2]

It is therefore not imperative to be able to project the exact level of interest rates at any particular point in time, but rather to properly position an institution's portfolio to maximize flexibility and return. There are two ways by which earnings can be generated. The first is by securing funds at a particular rate of interest and employing those funds at a yield in excess of the cost for a maturity identical with that of the source of funds. Both the asset and liability mature simultaneously and the funds made available by the maturing asset are used to repay the maturing liability. This process is repeated. If management wishes to increase earnings, a larger spread must be maintained between the cost of funds and the use of those funds, maintaining similar maturities in both cases. It is quite obvious that this technique would be impossible to employ over time, since assets with identical maturities and adequate spreads cannot be found for each dollar of liability and capital that enters the institution.

The second approach is to attempt to determine the impact on interest margins by mismatching the maturities between rate-sensitive assets and rate-sensitive liabilities. If management secures fixed-rate liabilities and employs them in floating rate assets during a period of rising interest rates, an increase in earnings on the floating rate asset is achieved, but no increase in liability costs on those fixed rate liabilities occurs. As a result, the net effect on earnings is positive.

Asset and Liability Positioning
In order to properly position an asset and liability portfolio, management must follow three steps: 1) Assets and liabilities must be classified as "rate-sensitive" or "non-rate-sensitive," specifying each asset's and liability's respective matu-

rity; 2) The interest rate yields (costs) and dollar volumes of each asset and liability account must be determined; 3) Management must develop the measurement tools for analyzing these data and a format for interpreting the results. Upon completion of these steps, management can interpret how the profitability of its asset and liability portfolio is impacted by interest rate movements. (These movements will have been previously determined in management's interest rate forecast.) Finally, with the analysis complete, adjustments in the asset and liability portfolio consistent with management objectives may be made. However, depending upon the present composition of the portfolio this may be a lengthy process.

Philosophical Approaches

Management can select one of three philosophical approaches in managing the asset and liability positions of their financial institutions. The first is an "aggressive approach" whereby management adopts a goal of increasing earnings by aggressively and deliberately mismatching its portfolio in an attempt to maximize its earnings. The second is a "defensive" approach whereby management attempts to minimize the interest rate exposure which could arise from the rapid and significant changes in interest rates. This approach attempts to protect net interest margins from unexpected or further erosion. The third is a "moderate risk" approach for those institutions not attempting to maximize earnings by actively mismatching funds nor attempting to defensively protect existing margins from further erosion. Regardless of the philosophical approach chosen by management, the rate sensitivity, maturity and dollar volume must be analyzed continuously in order for the policies of asset and liability management to be effective.

Interest Rate Sensitivity

Many balance sheet problems which have arisen over the last several years are due to the volatility of interest rates. Determining the degree that interest rate movements will affect profitability requires a classification of assets and liabilities based upon sensitivity to interest rates over various periods of time. Generally, rate-sensitive assets and liabilities are those that can be repriced within one year. Depending upon the need to increase flexibility and the ultimate ramifications of being unsuccessful, the timeframe over which one analyzes rate sensitivity is somewhat relative. One can analyze interest rate sensitivity on a monthly, quarterly, semi-annual, or annual basis.

Generally, those assets which are considered interest-rate sensitive would be: 1) floating rate loans; 2) loans maturing; 3) investments maturing; and 4) fixed-rate loan amortization/payoffs.[3] Maturing investments such as Federal Funds, money market assets, government securities, and municipal securities which will mature during the designated period and will be reinvested at current market rates, should be considered interest-rate sensitive. Generally, interest-sensitive liabilities are defined as: 1) short-term borrowing; 2) maturing certificates of deposit and money market certificates; and 3) floating rate liabilities.[4]

It is also wise to analyze those asset and liability classifications that are non rate-sensitive at the present time, but which will become rate-sensitive as they approach maturity dates. Those non-interest rate sensitive assets which have a maturity beyond the time horizon chosen by management for their analysis should not be excluded, especially if those funds might not be reinvested in fixed-rate instruments. For example, if a package of fixed-rate mortgages (non-interest rate sensitive) were to be sold and the funds immediately reinvested in Federal Funds at current market rates, the analysis of interest-rate sensitivity would not result in optimal utilization of funds if these mortgage funds were not considered.

Figure 7-9 examines the interest-rate sensitivity of wholesale versus retail institutions. The wholesale institution has a portion of its rate-sensitivity assets financed with fixed-rate liabilities, while the retail institution has a portion of its non-rate-sensitive assets financed by rate-sensitive liabilities. As interest rates trend upward, the earnings for a wholesale institution increase as a result of its rate-sensitive asset portfolio.

For the retail institution, an increase in interest causes the liability cost of that institution to increase; however, a corresponding rise in asset income financed by the rate-sensitive liabilities does not occur. The net result is a decrease in earnings, such as seen in the savings and loan industry and some regional and local commercial banks that have been heavily invested in mortgages. In 1979, a mortgage at 9% based on a cost of funds of 6% resulted in a 3% margin. That mortgage in 1982 is yielding the same 9%, but the cost of funds has shifted to money-market rates at approximately 10 to 12 percent, resulting in a 1-3 percent negative spread on a portion of the institution's portfolio.

Classification

Figure 7-10 categorizes a financial institution's balance sheet into rate-sensitive assets and liabilities. Also within each rate-sensitive account classi-

Figure 7-9   Interest Rate Sensitivity

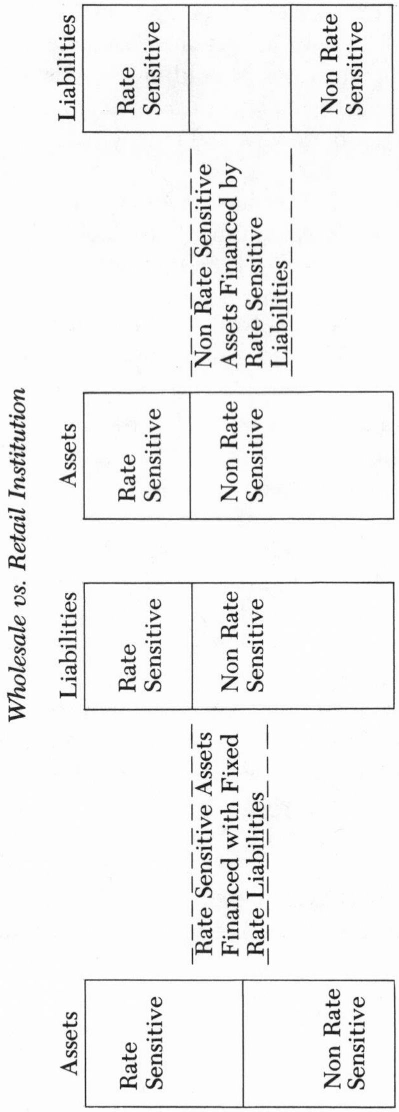

Wholesale vs. Retail Institution

Figure 7-10   Portfolio Interest Rate Sensitivity

December 31, 198X
($000)

Assets		Liabilities	
Rate Sensitive Assets—(RSA)		**Rate Sensitive Liabilities (RSL)**	
Short Term Investments	$10,000	Repurchase Agreements	$ 8,000
Taxable Securities:		Certificates of Deposit (100,000+)	
0–3 mo.	4,000	0–3 mo.	9,000
3–6 mo.	4,000	3–6 mo.	8,000
6–9 mo.	3,000	6–9 mo.	5,000
9 mo.–1 yr.	4,000	9 mo.–1 yr.	6,000
Non Taxable Securities		Money Market Certificates	
0–3 mo.	3,000	0–3 mo.	5,000
3–6 mo.	4,000	3–6 mo.	8,000
6–9 mo.	3,000	6–9 mo.	7,000
9 mo.–1 yr.	2,000	9 mo.–1 yr.	8,000
Commercial Loans (Fixed)		All Savers Certificates	
0–3 mo.	3,000	0–3 mo.	8,000
3–6 mo.	8,000	3–6 mo.	4,000
6–9 mo.	6,000	6–9 mo.	4,000
9 mo.–1 yr.	8,000	9 mo.–1 yr.	6,000
Commercial Loans (Variable)	30,000	IRA Accounts	
Other RSA[1]	-0-	0–3 mo.	3,000
Total RSA	**$ 92,000**	3–6 mo.	1,000
Non Rate Sensitive Assets-(NRSA)		6–9 mo.	2,000
Mortgage Loans	30,000	9 mo.–1 yr.	4,000
Installment Loans	15,000	Other RSL[2]	-0-
Total Earning Assets	**137,000**	**Total RSL**	**96,000**
Non Earning Assets—(NEA)		Remaining Interest-Bearing Liabilities:	41,000
Cash and Due	5,000		
Furn./Fixtures/Equip.	3,000	Non Interest-Bearing Liabilities:	8,000
Building/Land	5,000		
Total Non Earning Assets	**13,000**	Capital/Surplus/ Undivided Profit	13,000
Total Assets	**$150,000**		
		Total Liabilities Plus Capital	**$150,000**

[1] Other RSA
[2] Other RSL—Floating Rate Notes/Bonds

fication, three-month time intervals are used as periods within which the asset and liability account items will be replaced, somewhat refining the rate-sensitivity even further.

In terms of rate-sensitive assets, the example includes short-term investments of $10 million, primarily, Federal Funds which can be sold on an overnight basis. During 1980, the rate paid on Fed Funds sold ranged from 14% to 16% with an average maturity of between 1 and 3 days. Fifteen million dollars of taxable securities were U.S. government and agency securities maturing quarterly through the year. Non-taxable securities totaling $12 million were primarily state and local funds (municipal securities.)

Fixed-rate commercial loans which mature throughout the year total $25 million (nearly half mature within six months). Variable-rate commercial loans total $10 million. There were no other rate-sensitive assets; however, if fixed-rate consumer loans, mortgage loans, or student loans had included amounts which would be amortized or paid off during the year, and which could be reinvested at current market rates, these would have been classified as interest-rate sensitive and would have been included in this classification.

This institution has $92 million of its $150 million total asset portfolio in interest-rate sensitive assets. Fixed-rate mortgages total $30 million, while non-variable installment loans total $15 million. Non-earning assets, including cash and due, equipment and premises, and building and land total $13 million.

Among rate-sensitive liabilities, the repurchase agreement portfolio contains contracts which mature daily, and can be repriced accordingly. These total $8 million. A total of $28 million in negotiable certificates of deposit, those being in excess of $100,000, mature within the year in question. Of this total, $9 million mature within the first three months of the year; $28 million of money market certificates also mature quarterly in the year. All-savers certificates maturing during this period total $22 million and can be repriced, while $10 million of floating-rate 1 1/2-year IRA certificates also mature systematically throughout the year. In this example, no other rate-sensitive liabilities such as variable-rate bonds exist. This institution has $95 million in rate-sensitive liabilities. The remaining interest-bearing liabilities which are not rate-sensitive total $41 million, being comprised of $22 million in savings accounts, $8 million in NOW accounts, Golden Premium or other time accounts, and $8 million in non-interest bearing liabilities.[5] Capital surplus and undivided profits total $13 million for a grand total of $150 million dollars in total liabilities and capital.

These data can be reexamined in a number of ways to determine the financial institution's position relative to the degree of impact selected changes in interest rates will have on it. Generally, if given an increasing trend in rates, the financial institution would prefer having a greater proportion of its assets in interest-sensitive assets rather than in interest-sensitive liabilities. Under the same forecast, the institution would also prefer reducing the maturity of its asset portfolio while expanding the maturity of its liability portfolio. However, if the interest rate forecast is for declining interest rates, the institution would prefer to have a larger proportion of its liabilities in interest-sensitive liabilities rather than in interest-sensitive assets, and would prefer increasing the maturity on its assets and decreasing the maturing on its liability portfolio. Keep in mind, that if interest-sensitive assets are funded by interest-sensitive liabilities, and non-interest sensitive assets are funded with non-interest sensitive liabilities, the institution is not subject to interest rate risk. On the other hand, if interest-sensitive assets are funded by non-interest sensitive liabilities, or non-interest sensitive assets are funded with interest-sensitive liabilities, the institution becomes subject to interest rate risk.

Rate Sensitivity Analysis

Figure 7-11 provides summary data in a format which allows management to analyze their financial position. For each three-month interval, rate-sensitive assets and liabilities are listed along with a computation providing the difference between rate-sensitive assets and rate-sensitive liabilities. The resulting surplus or deficiency in interest-sensitive assets and/or liabilities can be reviewed. Rates of rate-sensitive assets to rate-sensitive liabilities provide relative measures of the asset/liability composition and a basis for reviewing

Figure 7-11 Interest Sensitivity Measurement

($ Millions)

	3 mo.	6 mo.	9 mo.	1 yr.
RSA	$50	$66	$78	$92
RSL	$33	$54	$72	$96
RSA—RSL	$17	$12	$ 6	$ 4
RSA/RSL	1.52	1.22	1.08	.96
RSA/TA	.33	.44	.52	.61
RSL/TL	.13	.23	.33	.66

trends. Figure 7-11 reveals that within the first three months of the year under analysis, the rate-sensitive asset position of this institution totals $50 million, while the rate-sensitive liability position totals $33 million, resulting in a surplus rate-sensitive asset position of $17 million, or a rate sensitivity ratio of 1.52. This means that this institution is positioned more positively to operate under a near term rising interest rate scenario. For any given increase in interest rates, the returns on the asset portfolio will be 50% greater than the cost of the liability portfolio.

If one looks at the one-year time horizon in total, however, a slightly different perspective can be derived. The rate-sensitive asset position of $92 million is below the rate-sensitive liability position of $96 million, resulting in a surplus rate-sensitive liability position for the year of $4 million or a sensitivity ratio of 0.96%. This reflects a financial position that would not benefit from an increasing interest rate scenario over the one-year period but could benefit from decreased rates. For every percentage increase in interest rates, this institution would experience a decrease in net interest margins.

One could also compute ratios of the rate-sensitive assets to total assets or total earning assets, or the rate-sensitive liabilities to total liabilities. These measures indicate assets or liabilities capable of being repriced in relation to the total investment position or liability base of the institution.

Maturity Matching

One of the primary objectives of asset and liability management is to match maturities of rate-sensitive assets and liabilities in order to provide a self-liquidating vehicle whereby funds from maturing assets could supply the funds required to cover maturing liabilities. Within the discipline of finance, there is an axiom that states that short-term assets should be financed with short-term liabilities, and long-term assets with long-term liabilities, given, of course, a positive interest spread between the cost of funds and the return on funds.

Perfect matching of maturities in similar dollar denominations is not possible and several problems can arise. First, a mismatching may require additional funds to support liquidating liabilities if the length of asset maturities exceeds that of the liabilities which funded those particular assets. Second, reduced or even negative short-term yields or spreads between assets and liabilities may take place as a result of disintermediation when an inverted yield curve exists. Periods such as 1966, 1969–1970, 1973–1975, and 1979–1981 resulted in increased volatility and short-term interest rates above long-term interest rates. Management could maintain maximum flexibility by stressing matched maturities so that within any given period the amount of funds needed for refunding liabilities would spontaneously arise from the maturing assets. Profitability requires maintaining positive net interest rate spread between the yield on assets and the cost of liabilities funding those assets.

A portion of Figure 7-12 analyzes the maturity matching for a financial institution over a three-month period. This particular institution has a total of $60 million in assets funded during this 90-day period of $60 million of liabilities (a "laddering" investment approach.)

It has $10 million maturing in 30 days with $20 million maturing in 60

Figure 7-12   Maturity Gap and Yield Spread Analysis

Assets

($000) Amount	% of Total	Maturity	Weighted Factor	Yield	Weighted Factor
10,000	16.67	30 day	5.00	10.0	1.67
20,000	33.33	60 day	20.00	10.5	3.50
30,000	50.00	90 day	45.00	11.0	5.50
$60,000	100.00		70 days		10.67%

$$\text{Weighted Ave. Maturity } (WAM_a) = 70 \text{ days}$$
$$- \text{ Weighted Ave. Maturity } (WAM_l) = 57.5 \text{ days}$$
$$\text{GAP/Maturity Mismatch} \quad \underline{12.5 \text{ days}}$$

Liabilities

($000) Amount	% of Total	Maturity	Weighted Factor	Cost of Funds	Weighted Factor
20,000	33.33	30 day	10.00	8.0	2.67
25,000	41.67	60 day	25.00	8.5	3.54
15,000	25.00	90 day	22.50	9.0	2.25
$60,000	100.00		57.50 days		8.46

$$\text{Weighted Ave. Yield } (WAY_a) = 10.67\%$$
$$- \text{ Weighted Ave. Cost of Funds } (WAC_l) = 8.46\%$$
$$\text{Net Interest Margin/Spread} \quad \underline{2.21\%}$$

days and $30 million maturing in 90 days. In 30 days, $20 million in liabilities come due with $15 million maturing in 60 days and $10 million maturing in 90 days.

GAP Analysis

In an attempt to evaluate the GAP or maturity imbalance between asset and liability portfolios, a time period for analysis must be chosen. It is imperative to note that the results from such an examination may vary tremendously, based upon the time periods selected for analysis. In Figure 7-12, a weighted average maturity is computed for both assets and liabilities by taking the proportion of assets and liabilities maturing within each of the 30-day intervals as a percent of total assets and liabilities, and multiplying that percentage by the number of days to maturity, to develop a weighted time factor. These weighted factors are then summed to determine an overall weighted average maturity for both assets and liabilities. In terms of assets, this institution has $10 million, or 16.7% of its total asset portfolio maturing with 30 days, resulting in a weighted factor of 5 days. Within 60 days, $20 million or one-third of its asset portfolio matures, resulting in a weighted factor of 20 days, while $30 million or 50% of the asset portfolio matures within 90 days, resulting in a weighted factor of 45 days. The summation of the 5 day, 20 day, and 45 day factors results in a weighted average maturity of 70 days. By computing a similar liability portfolio factor and taking the difference, a net "gap" or maturity imbalance in this institution's asset and liability portfolio can be seen. In this instance, a positive gap of 12.5 days results.

Any difference in weighted average maturities between assets and liabilities could result in pressures on profitability due to changing interest rate trends. On the average, in our example the cost of funds would increase for 12.5 days without resulting in increased asset yields to support the additional cost of funds.

It should be noted that this analysis is somewhat oversimplified in that for any given change in interest rates, the assets and liabilities may not be instantaneously affected. The types of assets and liabilities will affect the reaction to a given change, say in prime interest rate. In terms of decreasing interest rates, for example, certain liability costs tend to decrease faster than the yields on certain assets. Management must closely examine the composition of the balance between sources and uses of funds by maturity.

In terms of the assets and liabilities maturing within 30 days, it should be noted that $10 million assets will be maturing within 30 days, while $20 million in liabilities will mature within 30 days; therefore management should begin evaluating potential sources for an additional $10 million to fund the maturing liabilities. This institution may have to enter the short-term money market and competitively bid for an additional $10 million in funds to support the maturing liabilities or convert a portion of its liquid asset portfolio. Within 60 days, there will be a $5 million deficiency and by the 90th day, $30 million in assets will mature, while only $15 million in liabilities will mature.

If the assets mature before the liabilities, or the absolute dollar amount of assets exceeds the dollar amount of liabilities maturing, the refunding situation incurs interest rate risk. Depending upon the level and trend of interest rates, it may be more beneficial to have a positive *or* negative gap. Assume for instance, that interest rates decline. Because of the shorter maturity in the liability portfolio, liabilities will be repriced at a lower rate, on the average 12.5 days sooner than the assets mature, and this would add to the overall profitability of the organization.

Net Interest Spread/Net Interest Margin
If one is interested in determining a margin of profit generated on the asset and liability portfolio, a similar weighted average computation on asset yield and liability cost of funds should be conducted. By taking the percentage of the asset and liability portfolios maturing within each of the three time periods specified in Figure 7-12, and multiplying that percentage by the expected yield, a weighted factor can be computed. When these factors are summed, a weighted average yield for the asset and liability portfolio is obtained. Subtracting the weighted average cost of funds from the weighted average yield on the asset portfolio reveals a yield spread and net interest margin:

Net Profit Margin = Weighted Yield - Weighted Cost

$$2.21 = 10.67 - 8.46$$

This net interest margin is that margin of profit which must cover all other operating expenses and provide a net profit to stockbrokers. In this particular instance, the weighted average asset yield is 10.67%, while the weighted average cost of funds is 8.46%, resulting in a net interest margin of 2.21%. The higher the net interest margin, the larger the cushion for expense coverage available to an institution. Net interest income provides the basis for covering the financial institution's "burden," which is defined as non-interest expense minus non-interest income.

Rate Volume Analysis

In addition to net interest margin, an analysis of net interest spread is often conducted by financial institutions to examine the interest spread between the yield on earning assets and the cost of interest-bearing liabilities. This analysis can be computed on a monthly basis by taking the monthly income from earning assets and dividing it by the average daily balance of those assets, resulting in a yield on earning assets. The interest expense incurred for a particular month is divided by the average daily balance of the interest-bearing liabilities. The difference between the yield on earning assets and the cost on interest-bearing liabilities is called interest rate spread.

Rate, Volume, and Mix

Note that rate, volume, and mix should be analyzed in order to effectively manage an asset and liability portfolio. If one were to manage an asset and liability portfolio of $1 million each, and the yield on the asset portfolio was 10% and the cost of funds on the liability portfolio was 8%, the maturity on the asset portfolio was 30 days, while the maturity on the liability portfolio was 60 days, a decline in interest rates would result in a lower yield on the asset portfolio being repriced 30 days before the liability portfolio matures. This ultimately would result in a lower net interest margin. If the liability portfolio doubled in size and the funds were invested in assets with similar maturities of 30 days, the net interest margins over the next 60 days would be squeezed that much more significantly. Consequently, if interest rates were increasing within a short period of time similarly to what transpired from August 1979 to mid-November 1979, and August 1980 to December 1980, when interest rates increased 375 basis points and 850 basis points respectively, the profit margins from an asset and liability portfolio with such a gap would be to the advantage and benefit of the institution.

Hedging/Arbitrage

If one structures the volume and mix of the asset and liability portfolio so that both sides of the balance sheet are equally affected by interest rate movements, the net interest margin will remain relatively unaffected. This approach is considered to be a type of hedging or a method of arbitrage to protect profit margins. Primarily, hedging relates to a defensive approach to asset and liability management, where interest rate margins are protected and maintained. In an aggressive or speculative approach, asset and liability portfolios are purposely mismatched in an attempt to capitalize on interest rates and maturity imbalances. For some institutions, managing the maturity gap and the net interest margin is sufficient to minimize interest rate exposure. By definition, perfectly matching asset and liability maturities is a type of arbitrage whereby an institution uses funds based on a predetermined spread between the marginal cost of funds and the marginal returns on the assets financed by those respective liabilities.

Some institutions have begun to analyze the possibilities of futures contracts to hedge against adverse movements in interest rates based on their own asset and liability position. Much has been written about futures contracts and the differentiation between hedging and speculation, and a great deal of the regulatory pressure exerted in the recent past has evolved around this specific point. There is a fine line between speculation and hedging, and the regulatory agencies have been extremely apprehensive about the speculative aspects of futures contracts. The concern has been whether or not a bank could defer gains or losses on futures contracts to use as a hedge on a cash instrument, and whether those gains or losses could be rolled into the interest income or expense of an instrument. Banking regulators insist that such futures positions be marked to market, and that losses be realized in the current reporting period regardless of whether the hedge continues beyond them. Regulatory authorities have commented that they would accept a concept of deferral from one reporting period to the next on the net balance sheet hedge. The regulatory rules still prohibit hedge accounting for deferral of gains or losses on the call report every bank must submit to them. Because of the newness of the futures concept, relative to non-commodity items, such as interest-related securities, institutions should be extremely careful in their use of futures contracts for anything but pure hedging purposes. The losses which could be incurred by mismanagement of futures applications could be significant, and could have extremely adverse consequences on overall profitability, not to mention the safety and solvency of the organization. As research continues in this area, the utilization of financial futures will more than likely increase in popularity, especially if interest rate volatility continues through of the 1980s.

NOTES

[1] George J. Vojta, *Bank Capital Adequacy*, First National City Bank of New York, 1973, p. 31.

[2] Ronald L. Olson, Donald G. Simonson, Stanley R. Reber, and George H. Hampel, "Management of Bank Interest Margins in the 1980's", *Magazine of Bank Administration*, March 1980, p. 33.

[3] Any loan or investment maturing, as well as any run-off or pay-off, which would provide funds that would be reinvested at the current market rate would be considered rate-sensitive. Funds derived from fixed-rate loans or below market investments such as municipal securities, which would be reinvested in the same account classification at below current market rates, would not be considered interest rate-sensitive.

[4] A 20-year floating rate money center bank bond would be an example of a liability which would fall into this classification.

[5] Note that if the DIDC develops a "Super NOW" Account and/or allows financial institutions to operate sweep-money fund accounts, the interest sensitivity of the institutions will change significantly.

8

The Strategic Planning Director

This chapter analyzes the role and responsibility of the Board of Directors. Some of these responsibilities involve strategic planning, some involve the overall operations and financial control of the bank. Without a purpose and mission for the bank, the Board of Directors will find it extremely hard to meet all the objectives and goals of the bank, while concurrently operating in a safe and solvent manner.

General Responsibilities

Duty of Care. Every member of the Board of Directors has the responsibility of the duty of care. This means that all directors must be responsible for their activities and the activities of others employed by the commercial bank. They will be diligent and vigilant to the financial and operational facets of the commercial bank. They cannot be negligent to the general responsibilities of their job as members of the Board of Directors. The duty of care is primarily a common law standard, and as such is extremely vague and ambiguous. What it really means is that the members of the Board of Directors must participate actively in the work of the Board of Directors, question possible illegal and/or unethical activities, assure themselves that all financial arrangements are safe and solvent, make sure that all employees of the commercial bank operate in a legal and ethical manner, and that all regulatory, securities, and corporate activities are within the laws and regulations imposed upon the commercial bank. The lack of attendance at meetings, participation at meetings, preparation for the meetings, voicing one's opinion, taking a stand when one believes that there is a serious managerial or financial problem within the commercial bank, and other inaction or lack of care situations indicate potential problems for any members of the Board of Directors. Since the duty of care is by far the hardest to define and thus to implement, it is also the easiest to violate. A member of the Board of Directors may not know that he or she is violating the duty of care until it is too late, and thus if the director does not believe that he or she is pursuing all facets of the job as a member of the Board of Directors, that member should immediately resign from the board.

Duty of Loyalty. Every member of the Board of Directors of a commercial bank owes his or her loyalty to the institution. This is classified as a general responsibility, because it transcends every specific duty and responsibility that any director has. The duty of loyalty runs the gamut from mere confidentiality of any information received in his or her capacity as a member of the Board of Directors to reporting situations where members of the Board of Directors deliberately convey information to other financial institutions which may adversely affect the financial performance of his or her bank. In addition, if members of the Board of Directors cannot actively participate in the general business of the bank that they serve they are violating the duty of loyalty to the institution. Since F.I.R.A., there are often constraints placed on members of the Board of Directors to do all their business with their own bank. There are reforms pending in Congress to tone down the general bias against members of the Board of Directors and the extreme disclosure burden placed upon them. Those of you who may be doing business with more than one financial institution in order to bypass today's disclosure requirements may find comfort within a year or two. Acts of disloyalty towards your commercial bank may consist of bad-mouthing your bank in front of friends, customers, or the citizenry in general, as well as by not participating actively in the affairs of the bank. The latter is an implicit way of being disloyal to the responsibility that you have undertaken on behalf of the stockholders.

Policy Formulation. If anything is missing in the commercial bank Board of Directors, it is the lack of general and specific policy formulation, which is then implemented by the professional management of the commercial bank into procedures to operate the commercial bank. Many commercial banks operate with no idea of what the future holds, where the commercial bank fits into the local banking market, or what steps must be taken in order to improve banking services, improve profitability, improve competency of staff, and meet all of the increasingly complex uncertainties of the current banking environment. It is not infrequent for the Board of Directors to gather together on a bi-monthly or monthly basis to examine certain specific items such as past-due loans, classified assets, branch and/or main building modernizations, and to review the monthly financial statements, while at the same time never analyzing thorough strategic planning, budgetary analysis, or other policy formulations and procedures or policies to dictate the future course of the commercial bank. Thus, one of the most important general responsibilities of any member of the Board of Directors of a commercial bank is to participate in the formulation of the policies that will dictate the course of the activities of the bank so that it may proceed to bring a fair return to its shareholders, and to participate actively in the banking market in which it is located.

Overall Financial Control. A commercial bank is a financial institution that handles cash, demand and time deposits, and loads and loads of credit. Financial institutions are more susceptible to embezzlement and misappropriation of funds since their inventory is money or its near substitutes. It is extremely important for members of the Board of Directors to understand that one of their major responsibilities is to assure the safe and solvent operation of the commercial bank, and to implement the policies and to provide the necessary personnel, either internal or external, to assure the general financial solvency and stability of the bank. Since most members of the Board of Directors are not professional accountants, financial analysts, or associated specifically in the money and banking areas, it is necessary for the Board of Directors to delegate the overall financial and audit control of the commercial bank to competent professional personnel. The days when members of the Board of Directors could do their own bank directors' examinations, and could certify to either the state or federal regulatory agencies that the books were in a safe and solvent condition, are gone. Computerization of the records, complexity of the federal and state regulations and statutes under which commercial banks operate, and the everchanging, complex world of banking make it almost impossible for any normal Board of Directors to handle the financial and audit control of the bank by themselves. This is true regardless of whether the bank is $10 million in size or over several billion dollars. Hence, it is necessary for the Board of Directors to provide the resources necessary, either internally or externally, to provide the safeguards for overall financial and audit control.

There are two major facets of overall financial and audit control that are important. The first is to develop the accounting system necessary to factually and accurately represent the financial condition and performance of the commercial bank. Bank examinations simply review the present controls available, and analyze the shortcomings of the bank's performance. They do not establish the financial accounting procedures and controls necessary for safe and solvent operation. On the other hand, auditing the records of the commercial bank is a separate, and equally important, function of the Board of Directors. Its audits can be both internal and external, and often both are performed when the commercial bank reaches a size and is able to afford such external audits, as well as internal audits. There is a real danger of having only internal audits, especially when the commercial bank is so small that there is only one internal auditor, one employee responsible for analyzing and ferreting out all internal irregularities and procedures, controls, and illegal activities. Over the past ten years we have been involved in commercial bank situations on over a dozen occasions where the source of the embezzlements or internal misappropriation of funds was the internal auditor, rather than other officers or employees. Furthermore, this was primarily due to the ability of the internal auditor to make all the necessary arrangements within the bank for such embezzlement and/or misappropriation. The Board of Directors should consider carefully the use of external auditors, regardless of their cost, to act as a check and balance to an internal auditor. If internal auditors are used, such internal audit staff should be suprvised by the Board of Directors, and should report directly to the Board of Directors on anything found to be of a suspicious nature within the bank. Improvements in internal controls and procedures can then be delegated back to management for implementation, and accountability can be brought back to the Board of Directors. Since commercial banks are highly susceptible to embezzlement and/or misappropriation, this general responsibility of the Board of Directors is an extremely important one which cannot be ignored at any time.

Business Development. The Board of Directors should realize that the long-term existence of the commercial bank depends upon its ability to be able to maintain current business and to develop future business. Thus, one of the major responsibilities of the Board of Directors is to develop policies necessary to implement business development plans, and to participate actively in the business development process. As customers turn over, it is necessary to replenish the general business of the commercial bank. Failure to have devised business development plans to assist in such rejuvenation will in the long run mean the demise of the commercial bank. Thus, the Board of Directors should determine what plans are needed to assure the future growth of the commercial bank, delegate the business development policy for professional management to implement, and scrutinize the results of such policies.

Reviewability and accountability. Finally, another general responsibility should be noted. Too often the Board of Directors makes policy and then never finds out whether or not it has been implemented. Time and time again, professional management will let the Board of Directors have its way, develop policies, and then never implement them, knowing full well that the Board of Directors never ask for accountability. Thus, one of the major responsibilities of the Board of Directors is to make sure that all policies that have been delineated by the Board of Directors are implemented, or if not, the board should be informed of the reasons why such implementation was impossible. The Board of Directors should formulate procedures by which all policies delegated to management are brought back to the Board of Directors in a prescribed period of time for review. The accountability of professional management of the Board of Directors is extremely important in coordinating policy and procedural implementation. It permits the Board of Directors to keep the control of the commercial bank where it belongs—at the board level. In those cases where the commercial bank Board of Directors does not exercise review and accountability control, the commercial bank is usually run by the professional management, and the Board of Directors has subrogated its responsibilities to those of the professional management. This is a violation of their charge.

See Chapter 11 for detailed analysis of accountability and review as it pertains to strategic planning.

Specific Board Responsibilities

As a result of a general responsibilities outline, the Board of Directors of any commercial bank has certain specific duties and responsibilities. Although this book concentrates on the responsibility of the bank directors in regard to strategic planning, we have outlined all of the responsibilities in order for you to understand the entire scope of the specific responsibilities of the bank director.

Overall policy formulation. Since the shareholders have delegated the responsibility of the overall philosophy and policy formulation to the Board of Directors, one of the most important specific responsibilities of the Board of Directors is to formulate such overall philosophy and objectives. No two banks need to have the same philosophy, or the same objectives. But, it is vital for each commercial bank to have an established corporate philosophy, objectives, and goals toward which the management and employees can strive.

One of the most important functions of the Board of Directors is to formulate these overall philosophical policies. At the same time, it is necessary for the Board of Directors to stay out of the day-to-day operations of the bank. Once the policies and objectives have been outlined, it is up to management to implement them through established managerial procedures. It is not the responsibility of the Board of Directors to interfere with the everyday operation of the bank, but to review the efficacy of the policies implemented by management, and to assure the accountability and reviewability of such policies.

Definition of standards of conduct, ethical standards and other individual corporate policies. It is the directors' specific responsibility to outline standards of conduct and ethics not only for the management and employees, but also for the directors. It may seem easy to simply say, "Thou shalt not steal," but a specific code of conduct, code of ethics, or other standards of ethical consideration which are to be followed by all members of the corporate family, is far more effective than simple general platitudes. It is the responsibility of the Board of Directors to set the example, and standard for all to follow. The lack of doing so impacts unfavorably the overall ethics and standards of conduct of the employees of the bank.

Policy review and accountability. One of the most critical mistakes made regularly by the Board of Directors of commercial banks, and other corporations, is the lack of review and accountability of policy implementation. As we noted under general responsibilities, one of the major overall responsibilities of the Board of Directors is to make sure that the policies and procedures determined by the Board of Directors actually get implemented. Not only should they be implemented, but they should be analyzed for their effectiveness and if necessary they should be modified or cancelled. Thus, one of the most specific responsibilities of the Board of Directors is to set forth the procedures necessary for implementation of the board's policies and to constantly and regularly review, and, if necessary, cancel the policies. This is simply called the "sunset" illusion of corporate policy, similar to that found in many of the current federal and state laws. The Board of Directors should not consider that its policies, once implemented, should be any more efficient or helpful than any previously implemented policies. The Board of Directors should not only determine policy, but should delegate to management exactly when such policy should be implemented, and what review procedures must be undertaken in order to make sure that the management and the employees are accountable to the Board of Directors for each and every policy determined. As this is undertaken, it will be likely that professional management and the employees will implement policies determined by the Board of Directors far more efficiently than previously. And, more constant and regular review will permit the Board of Directors to ascertain whether or not such policies are beneficial to the overall operation of the financial institution. At the same time, constant review of policies determined by the Board of Directors allows them to assess whether the professional management has been accountable, and is another good indicator of the managerial performance of the senior management of the bank. Lack of implementation, lack of controls, and lack of review standards by professional management indicates to the Board of Directors that management is not as capable as indicated, and the Board of Directors may be forced to act accordingly.

Strategic planning. At the outset, strategic planning should be differentiated from overall policy formulation. Strategic planning is simply one policy that must be formulated. But it may be the most crucial responsibility that the Board of Directors accomplishes during its tenure. Strategic planning is the short-term and long-term planning for the survival of the financial institution. Strategic planning is the establishment of goals and objectives which encompass the master plan for the survival of the financial institution. In so doing, strategic planning becomes a major force in the overall operation of the commercial bank.

Although most of the members of the Board of Directors are not professional bankers, the strategic planning function is so vital to the preservation of the integrity of the financial institution that it becomes one of the most paramount functions and responsibilities of the Board of Directors. The board should not attempt to research and prepare the strategic plan by itself. It should, however, delegate the development of such planning, both short-term and long-term, to the professional management or an outside objective consultation firm approved by the Board of Directors, with subsequent review and accountability by the Board of Directors. In the long run, a commercial bank without a strategic plan will not survive. If it operates without a strategic plan, it simply operates from day-to-day, opening in the morning and closing in the evening, with no direct purpose. Strategic planning makes the overall operation of the banking institution worthwhile in the long run.

Composition of the Board of Directors. Proper composition of the Board of Directors is another major responsibility. Shareholders do not pick the members of the Board of Directors. The members of the Board of Directors pick their own colleagues. Thus, it is important to select appropriate, competent, efficient, and constructive members of the Board of Directors to assist in all of the facets of the operation of the commercial bank. Directors should be selected who can add to the overall expertise of the Board of Directors. Directors should represent all facets of community life, e.g., agricultural, labor, manufacturing, retail, homemakers, and other areas important to the local community. Keeping in mind that the Board of Directors of a commercial bank runs a for-profit business, the Board of Directors of the bank should be selected for their ability to contribute to the overall direction and leadership of the bank. The bank should not be considered as either a sorority/fraternity or country club. People should be selected to the Board of Directors for their ability to contribute, not for their name, prestige, wealth or social status, nor as a reward for their previous work on behalf of the community. Membership on a Board of Directors is not an honor; it is a responsibility. When a man or woman becomes a member of the Board of Directors of a commercial bank, he or she enters into a responsible position in which there are dangers of potential personal financial liability, as well as countless hours of stress and strain. Those selected for the Board of Directors should comprehend before accepting such a position that this job is one which expects future performance and is not a reward for past achievement. Directors should be selected to the Board of Directors on the basis of their ability and merit, not their wealth or scholastic background. Nepotism has no role to play on a competent Board of Directors unless the relation also happens to be the smartest individual in town. If someone does not meet up to the standards, he or she should be replaced by a competent individual to serve on the Board of Directors. The more challenging the atmosphere, the more stimulating the discussions, and thus the better direction the Board of Directors will provide the commercial bank.

Historically, directors may have been elected to the Board of Directors because of their significant depository, or more frequently, significant lending business with the commercial bank. Large depositor/borrower directors were felt to be akin to the responsible business persons of the community and often were sought by more than one commercial bank for membership on the Board of Directors. In the last four years, since the enactment of F.I.R.A., there has become a tendency for many business persons who have significant business with a commercial bank, to either resign from Boards of Directors or to refuse nomination to Board of Directors.

F.I.R.A. has eliminated some important and knowledgeable persons as candidates for the Board of Directors. These individuals do not wish to have their personal and/or corporate business arrangements with the commercial bank they serve placed in the open, while others within the bank who are not members of the Board of Directors remain anonymous. Furthermore, it seems incongruous that members of the Board of Directors should have to take their business to other commercial banks in order to remain anonymous.

When selecting members for the Board of Directors, it is necessary to instill into the potential directors the necessity for attendance at all meetings. Attendance at board meetings should be considered mandatory, not voluntary, and absence from board meetings does not relieve the directors from personal financial liability if acts of the bank incur such liability. Furthermore, extensive absences by members of the Board of Directors for personal vacations, Florida winter trips, and other business or social reasons should be grounds for elimination of a potential director: consideration submitted to the comptroller's office or to the Securities and Exchange Commission requires the name of any director who has missed more than 25 percent of the regularly scheduled board meetings during the previous year. Just another little stab at disclosure. It does indicate to the shareholders which directors are not participating actively in the affairs of the bank. Thus, to eliminate such problems, the directors of the bank should consider attendance mandatory. Finally, absence from the Board of Directors' meeting does not assist in the overall functioning of the board.

Compensation of directors is an important issue. The commercial bank is not a country club or a social fraternity; it is a business. The men and women who direct the business should be compensated equal to their responsibility as directors. Furthermore, the nature of the potential personal financial liability faced by members of the Board of Directors of a commercial bank is far more pervasive and significant than being a member of the Board of Directors of an ordinary industrial corporation. Such increased risk should also be compensated. Most commercial banks get what they pay for. If the members of the Board of Directors are not compensated in line with their responsibilities and liabilities, then the types of individuals who will sit on the Board of Directors will not be as strong as if they are adequately compensated.

Furthermore, the directors should be compensated in line with the amount of work required to be done, not the number of meetings attended. There is a tendency of directors to keep having meetings, especially if they are compensated per meeting, rather than getting the job done. Directors are selected and retained to assist in the policy formulation and control of the bank, and should be compensated by the year, not by the number of minutes, nor the number of times that they have to come to the bank for a meeting. This does not mean that there cannot be different compensation for different levels of responsibility on the Board of Directors. The Chairman of the Board certainly has more responsibility than other board members, and members of the Executive Committee or other regular standing committees may receive more compensation than other general directors of the bank. On the other hand, the directors should be paid a yearly stipend for their services. And if someone is not doing his or her job, he or she should be replaced by someone who will attend the meetings and participate. The historical reason for compensation by the meeting was to induce attendance. The fact that it induces attendance does not necessarily mean that it induces participation, leadership, direction, or other attributes of a good Board of Directors. It simply induces attendance, and if the individual is not interested in attending, he or she should be replaced with someone who is.

An issue of some importance to many commercial bankers is whether the Board of Directors should consist of predominantly outside directors, a majority of inside directors, or any other number of combinations. Inside directors, that is, professional management, have the expertise of being regular financially oriented business persons with a great deal of sophisticated, professional knowlege of what the bank is doing. Outside directors are normally not associated with banking institutions, and, thus, may not be as qualified in the area of finance as the professional inside directors. Inside directors, however, suffer from livelihood myopia. Members of the Board of Directors who are also professional managers are employees of the bank, and are responsible to the Board of Directors for their livelihood. There is a tendency for a pecking order to develop, especially when there is more than one inside director. Often they flock together like sheep. Thus, there is not much profiessional constructive criticism of ideas expressed in the meetings of the Board of Directors. Outside directors, although often not as knowledgeable in the financial area, have the ability to be dispassionate and objective, since they do not depend upon the commercial bank for their livelihood. They can be far more constructive, and can be much more objective to issues and problems arising at Board of Directors meetings. It would be naive to assume that they are unaware that they may not come back to the Board of Directors at the next annual meeting if they don't vote properly. So, there are some pressures even on the outside directors. But the pressures are obviously far less on outside directors than on inside directors.

A balance between inside and outside directors should be drawn in favor of the outside directors. Keeping in mind that professional management handles the operation of the financial institution, if professional management were in charge of the majority of the Board of Directors, there are possibilities, although remote, that unethical or illegal activities engaged in by management could be ratified by the Board of Directors unknowingly. Having a majority of the Board of Directors be outside directors, and not employees of the commercial bank, is another method of check and balance which will assist in alleviating some of the potential personal financial liability of the members of the

Board of Directors. We do not recommend the exclusion of professional inside management on the Board of Directors. To the contrary, it is of invaluable assistance to the entire Board of Directors for some members of the professional management to become members of the Board of Directors. In fact, more than one inside management should be on the Board of Directors, but the inside directors should never constitute a majority.

Most states require a minimum of five directors, and the regulations of the Comptroller of the Currency allow for a range of a minimum of five directors to a maximum of 25 directors. There is no magic number of directors, but it is most common to have an odd number of directors. Seven to nine directors is the norm for the industry. The number of directors should be in excess of five and the exact number of directors should be correlated to the size of the community, the market area to be served, and the number of generations necessary to cover the entire community in terms of an age spectrum. Too often Board of Directors are composed of elderly individuals, who may have been elected initially to the board 20 or 30 years ago, when they were much younger, but have not been either replaced or complemented by worthy individuals of the community as the original directors became older. Thus, it is not uncommon to find Board of Directors that do not represent the entire community, but only the older establishment of the community. The Board of Directors should fulfill its responsibility of representing the community by allowing a total number of directors who reflect the various age components of the community, as well as the various economic, social, financial, cultural, and religious segments of the community.

What the directors should do personally to fulfill their responsibility. The most important personal responsibility is preparedness. Directors can most assist in the policy formulation and overall direction of the bank by being prepared at all times, and especially at board meetings. This means that information must be made available to the directors, that they must be able to review such information prior to the meeting, and be fully conversant with all the information on the agenda. Obviously, attendance at the meetings is also required in order to be prepared and to be an integral part of the activities of the Board of Directors. If a director does not understand the material, he or she should consult professional management, the Chairman of the Board, or whoever is able to answer her or his questions prior to the meeting, so as not to take up time at the meeting. Failure to determine the answer to the problem or questions the director has prior to the meeting eliminates that director as an integral force in the determination of the policy proposed or the problem to be solved. Board members should take time to familiarize themselves with all the information prior to the meeting, and information should be made available at the bank prior to the meeting with sufficient time for it to be reviewed prior to the board meeting. There is no excuse for being unprepared. An unprepared director is no better than an absent director.

One of the major purposes for selecting certain people to the Board of Directors is to increase the status and prestige of the Board of Directors. The directors themselves can assist in the business development and marketing efforts of the bank by being excellent conduits within the community. Most directors are active community leaders, and as such, reflect the bank's image within the community. Directors also often have opportunities to exploit activities within the community to the bank's benefit. The Board of Directors should not be considered as part of the officer call program of the bank, but the Board of Directors should realize that one of their responsibilities is business development, and as such, an ability to be able to attract sound deposit and loan business to the bank should not be underestimated. A word of warning is necessary, however. Directors should solicit their friends, customers, and acquaintances and bring them to the bank. However, the Board of Directors should have the professional management determine the creditworthiness of individuals brought to the bank. The Board of Directors should not place undue pressure or influence upon professional management to give loans and/or other accommodation to individuals or businesses which are not creditworthy. The Board of Directors has marketing and business development responsibility, but it must keep its focus on the overall solvency and safety of the bank. In so doing, board members must permit the professional management to analyze and grade the credit of potential customers.

Independence of thought and action. Bank directors should not be drones or clones. A major responsibility of any member of the Board of Directors is to act independently and thoughtfully. The individual should not act destructively, or disruptively, within or outside the board meetings. No individual on the board, regardless of his or her age, marital status, sex, business position, or marital relationship with major shareholders, should act as a mouth-piece or stooge for any other director or shareholder. Remember, if there ever comes a time when your personal financial liability is on the line, you share the potential liability equally with the other members of the Board of Directors. The director cannot simply hide behind another director, saying that he or she was under the influence of Director A or B.

Furthermore, and even more important, a Board of Directors on which several directors do not actively participate, think independently, and provide constructive, alternative positions, is a Board of Directors which is hampered by the presence of stooges and dunces. The overall activities of the board suffer from the inability of all members to act constructively and independently on behalf of the shareholders. No director should be beholden to any particular group of shareholders, or directors. If a member of the Board of Directors cannot be independent, he or she should resign.

This responsibility is even more crucial when commercial banks are closely held. In come cases, an individual or a family may control over 50 percent of the bank. In such cases, the remainder of the Board of Directors may represent very few shareholders. There is a tendency in these types of situations for the minority directors to simply rubber stamp what the majority shareholder/director dictates. This can be fatal to the safety and solvency of the bank and all shareholders. If you are faced with one of these situations, and you cannot rectify it, it is best to look for some other means of entertaining yourself several hours a month. Your liability from a personal financial standpoint is equal dollar for dollar with that of the closely held majority shareholder/director, and there is no comfort to be had that he or she controls over 50 percent of the bank. If you cannot participate actively, constructively criticize the majority shareholder/director, and be an independent source within the commercial bank's Board of Directors, let someone else take your place on the Board of Directors and find something more constructive to do.

The responsibility of confidentiality. "Keeping one's mouth shut" or "not spilling the beans" is an important responsibility of any member of the Board of Directors. Most of the information received by the Board of Directors, be it financial or managerial in nature, is confidential information, and should not be spread around outside the bank. Several guidelines can assist the Board of Directors in meeting its responsibility of confidentiality. First of all, consider all information received by members of the Board of Directors as confidential, whether or not it is.

Second, the Board of Directors should discuss all information freely and completely within the confines of the board meeting. Information should not be discussed by members of the Board of Directors outside the board meeting, while still in the bank, or outside the bank building. One never knows who might be listening, and the information should be kept confidential in meetings between directors.

Finally, confidential information should never be used to solicit business by the members of the Board of Directors or professional staff. General bank information, especially public relations-oriented information, is perfectly appropriate for business solicitation purposes. The members of the Board of Directors should be absolutely sure that the information being used for business solicitation is not confidential information which would violate the confidentiality of any of the bank's customers.

Directors who have large mouths often cause bank problems. The Board of Directors should be concerned about leakage of financial information reports and other documents to the public, as well as leakage of conversations, inadvertently overheard. They should be most concerned about directors who deliberately, or unintentionally spread financial information concerning the commercial bank and/or its customers throughout the community. Directors have a responsibility to consider that all information received in the function as members of the Board of Directors must be kept confidential. Lack of confidentiality hurts the reputation of the bank, leaks information, and prohibits the bank from operating as efficiently as possible.

Disputations, conflicts of interest, and ethical considerations. Directors have a responsibility to be constructively critical, and to work according to their own understanding for the betterment of the bank. This does not mean that disputations will not take place; they will. But at the same time, if they are constructive, rather than wrangles, the bank will be served by the constructive disagreements and disputations.

The ethical conduct of the directors should not be subject to interpretation. If the reputation of any of the directors of a bank is tarnished, so is the bank. A member of the Board of Directors of a bank is in a very visible position, and indictments, threat of litigation, and unsubstantiated rumor may adversely affect the reputation of the bank. Furthermore, if it is discovered that the director has performed some questionable ethical practices, such as being disloyal to the institution, his or her behavior may have an impact on the directors and officers liability insurance and the ability of the bank to collect if damages have occurred. Every director should consider his or her job as a job of trust, and should always perform all duties in an ethical manner.

Directors should not deliberately get involved with conflicts of interest. Often, because of their professional and/or personal activities within the community, conflicts of interest do occur. When a director finds himself or herself in a potential conflict of interest, certain guidelines for meeting his or her responsibilities are as follows: 1) inform the board both orally and in writing of a possible conflict of interest; 2) disqualify oneself from voting on the item that presents the potential or actual conflict of interest; and 3) if the conflict is serious, the director should consult his or her own attorney. The director should know his or her own constitutional rights and simply stay away from deliberate conflicts of interest. What kind of conflicts can arise in the normal course of business? Let us assume that a major remodeling of the bank building is to be undertaken, and local builders will be asked to bid on the project. Is it a conflict of interest if one of the members of the Board of Directors, who happens to be a builder within the community, bids on the project? No, especially if the builder/director meets the same specifications and has to jump through all the same hoops that all the other bidders do. It certainly would be prudent for the builder/director not to be involved in the selection process, and if he or she wins the bid, it would be best for the bank management and the Board of Directors to document the reason for the winning bid in order to avoid questions of impropriety. This is not a conflict of interest, but could be one if handled improperly. Another example is one of the directors is in private business in the community, and one of his clients has a little problem with the bank. Can the director reveal to the Board of Directors that he has a financial interest or managerial interest in this other firm? Yes. This permits the entire Board of Directors to understand that this one director may have a conflict of interest, potential or real, arising from his or her different capacities within the community as a business person, director, or citizen. In this type of case, the director might wish to abstain from voting what to do with the business arrangement and to disqualify himself or herself of any possible conflict of interest.

Conflicts of interest arise more often than directors assume, and all directors should be aware that the normal duties of a bank director may conflict at times with the other activities of the director within the community. It may be virtually impossible for any director to avoid conflicts of interest, but revelation of such potential or actual conflicts of interest, and direct overt treatment of such conflicts will be in the best interests of the bank, the shareholders, and the remaining directors.

Retirement, resignation, and replacement of directors. Directors who have not lived up to standards should be replaced. We have found nothing in the banking rules and regulations, the National Banking Act, or the state statutes that says directors must not retire, and, therefore, they are able to die in their '80s with their boots on at a board meeting. Over the last decade, many commercial banks have installed mandatory retirement ages for directors, almost all of them equipped with grandfather clauses for present members of the Board of Directors. In 1973, an Ohio bank study commission survey indicated that the average age of bank directors at 275 Ohio state-chartered commercial banks was 74 years. The older the average age of the Board of Directors, the less representative it is of the community. The Board of Directors should regularly consider its own rejuvenation and replacement.

Individual directors should know when to retire or resign from the Board of Directors. They should not have to be forced out by a remainder of the Board of Directors. Replacement of directors is probably the hardest job that any director has to do. In fact, experience has indicated that it is easier for the Board of Directors to fire professional management than to replace one of their own on the Board of Directors. Replacement should be considered as an alternative for those directors who do not participate actively, are absent at meetings, and do not come prepared to meetings. However, replacement may not be necessary if the members of the Board of Directors realize that there is a time to get off as well as a time to get on the Board of Directors.

A director should retire when he or she is either physically or mentally incapable of doing the job. If the director cannot physically make it to the meetings, due to a stroke, heart attack or other physical ailment, or if the director has become mentally incompetent, the director should retire or resign from the Board of Directors. This director will have absolutely no input into the activities of the board, and his or her absence from the board may be a liability to the bank. The director should automatically and voluntarily resign or retire from the board and be replaced by someone who can devote full attention to the responsibility.

A director should resign if he or she is no longer interested in the job as a director and does not attend meetings. As a director becomes older, and he or she slows down in his or her business or other activities within the community, it may become relatively easy for the director to lose interest in a former commitment that was valuable. When a director seems to drift away, misses meetings, and really doesn't care, that is the time for the director to voluntarily resign or retire from the board with honors, before he or she must be replaced. Directors should resign when they believe that someone else could do the job better, and, thus, they should retire for purposes of being replaced by someone who will be more committed to the responsibility of being a bank director.

It is time to resign or retire when the director no longer lives within the community on a fulltime basis. Potential liability does not escape the director if the director is simply out of town. The director is potentially liable whether he or she is actively engaged in the board's activities or not. For those directors who decide to retire in Florida or Arizona, or who move out of town for three to six-month periods annually, it is time to be replaced by directors who will give a fulltime commitment to the direction of the bank. The winding down of one's own career within a community indicates a lack of interest in the affairs of the community, including the bank, and the person should be replaced on a voluntary basis by someone who will give fulltime attention to the activities of the bank.

Finally, if all other voluntary means fail, the Board of Directors should consider the replacement of absent and noncaring directors. Since the Board of Directors nominates itself, and the shareholders merely ratify the Board of Directors of a commercial bank, a recalcitrant, uncaring, absent director can be replaced simply by lack of renomination. This replacement function is difficult for most Boards of Directors. Directors should consider replacing an average or below average director with a competent director to be an important function, protecting themselves against potential liability, rather than as a violation of the code of care of the social fraternity. The Board of Directors operate a business, not a social club or fraternity, and directors who do not operate as full-fledged directors should be replaced by those who will.

Recruitment and retention of competent management. Members of the Board of Directors are not professional managers. In fact, most of them are not professional bankers. Therefore, it is extremely important for the Board of Directors to recruit and retain competent professional management. The better the management, the less the risk of potential personal financial liability accruing to the Board of Directors. It is the responsibility of the Board of Directors to hire and fire the professional management of the bank, and only through fulfilling this responsibility can the commercial bank be operated efficiently. The Board of Directors should not be satisfied with less than capable management, and it is essential to recruit, retain, and evaluate appropriate management. It is important to compensate management appropriately. The Board of Directors should not skimp on salaries and fringe benefits in order to try to save a few pennies here and there, since lack of competent management costs the bank more than just a few dollars.

Another important aspect of this responsibility is the review of the professional managers' performance. Since the Board of Directors annually elects the officers, and can replace them on a moment's notice, the Board of Directors must undertake a constructive review of the performance of the professional management. Guidelines used in assessing managerial performance of the officers include analysis of the financial statements, the financial performance of the commercial bank, the quality of the asset and liability portfolios, supervisory agency examination reports, strategic planning and policy formulation, and interpersonal relationships. There is no one else available to assess the management other than the Board of Directors, and it is their responsibility to do this job constructively and thoroughly in order to have the quality and competency of management necessary to have the bank perform at its ultimate.

Thus, the Board of Directors' responsibilities—general and specific—are major ones, and the body politic responsible for the planning of the future course of the bank, and the inability of the Board of Directors to perform its function may necessitate eventual liquidation and/or merger of the institution.

9

Management's Role In Strategic Planning

This chapter outlines what management has to do to assist in the strategic planning process. From an implementation standpoint, the role of management is exactly the same whether there is a strong Board of Directors or whether the bank is management oriented with the Board of Directors following quietly. However, if the Board of Directors is a force in strategic planning, the amount of leadership exercised by the management will be less than in any management-oriented commercial bank. In this chapter, we will analyze both types of management roles with emphasis on checks and balances between management and the Board of Directors. The ultimate objective is to increase the efficiency of the strategic planning process for the benefit of the board, management, employees, and shareholders of the commercial bank.

Management: Hand Maidens to the Board of Directors

Under corporate democracy, the Board of Directors is the elected group of individuals that is responsible to the shareholders. The shareholders, on a regular basis, elect the Board of Directors and under certain circumstances may fire the Board of Directors. The Board of Directors has a responsibility to the shareholders for the overall performance, safety, and solvency of the corporation, whether it be a commercial bank or any other type of corporation. The Board of Directors delegates the day-to-day operation of the corporation to the professional management. In some industries, such as commercial banking, professional management and the Board of Directors may be the same individuals. In some cases, also, the Board may be the majority stockholder of the commercial bank. Regardless, the professional management serves at the pleasure of the Board of Directors. Each year at the organization meeting following the shareholders meeting, the Board of Directors appoints the management for the ensuing year. In most jurisdictions, and under most circumstances, management which is not operating satisfactorily may be fired with or without cause. In case of illegal and/or illicit activities, the management may be suspended and/or fired immediately. In other cases, where employment contracts are involved, the management members may be fired individually or in toto under appropriate circumstances.

In a nut shell, the management works with the Board of Directors. This is just as true in strategic planning as it is in the operation of the bank. Thus, the management should perform all the duties necessary to meet the objectives and goals of the Board of Directors. It should be noted, however, that in most circumstances the Board of Directors will delegate the development of general and specific strategic plans to the management for its recommendation to the Board of Directors.

It cannot be overstated that the Board of Directors is not an everyday managerial unit of the commercial bank. The Board of Directors is a policy-making and decision-making body. Management is the body politic delegated to the performance of the everyday operation of the bank. Without cooperation between management and the Board of Directors, strategic planning will fail because the checks and balances system won't work.

The Board In Charge

Let us examine for a moment the scenario in which there is a strong Board of Directors and competent professional management. Here the Board of Directors understands its role as a planning body and acts as the overall policy-making constituency of the bank. In this particular case, the strategic planning process would be initiated by the Board of Directors, and delegated to the management to fulfill the development of the plans for the board to approve. Professional management may do the job internally or with the assistance of outside professional consultants.

It should be noted that the Board of Directors, in this situation, should outline as specifically as possible, exactly what strategic planning should be undertaken, the parameters of the reports to be returned to the Board of Directors, and the recommendations from the professional management for the development and implementation of such plans. Although this format is relatively rare, an increasingly large number of commercial bank boards are becoming aware of their responsibilities, and thus are charging the professional management with the preparation of strategic plans for the approval of the Board of Directors.

The Management In Control

The opposite situation from having the board in charge is when the management is in control of the banking organization. This means that the Board of Directors is either weak, or is rampant with professional management. This situation can take place in closely-held banks where the professional management is both the Board of Directors and the shareholder base. Although this format is undesirable, it is the most predominant form of bank direction and control. The following example demonstrates what can happen.

In this situation, management is still the professional management and subject to the dictates of the Board of Directors. Since the Board of Directors is not a strong body politic, and since they do not have an idea of where the bank should go, it is the obligation of the professional management, especially the Chief Executive Officer, to develop a recommended strategic plan for the commercial bank. In this type of organization, the professional management will determine what strategic planning must be done, develop the strategic plans internally (or use outside consultants to assist them), and present the reports to the Board of Directors. This process should be done properly to protect the fiduciary liability of both management and the Board of Directors, and so that all strategic planning is done under proper auspices, whether director-controlled or management-controlled.

Management's Responsibility to the Board of Directors

Regardless of whether the board has initiated the strategic planning or whether the management has initiated the planning process, it is the management's responsibility to the Board of Directors to make sure the job is done appropriately. This means that the job should be done to determine the strategic planning course of the institution, as well as cover all of the individual facets sufficiently so that the strategic plan has a probability of success and is within the constraints of the commercial bank's ability to perform the strategic plan. After delegation from the Board of Directors, or upon its own initiative, the management should undertake a scientific analysis of the strategic planning process and develop a plan that is logically cohesive and covers all the necessary areas.

Initiators of the Strategic Planning Policies
It is important to note that there must be a catalytic agent in order for the planning process to work. This means that there must be an initiator for the strategic planning process. This role is normally performed by management. Even in those commercial banks where there is a strong Board of Directors, management typically initiates the strategic planning discussion, even if it has not provided preliminary recommendations. Thus, it is the role of management to initiate the strategic planning process within the constraints and delegated powers laid down by the Board of Directors.

Management's Responsibility and Accountability to the Board of Directors for Implementation
One of management's major responsibilities to the Board of Directors is accountability for the implementation of the strategic planning program. After its development and approval by the Board of Directors, the strategic planning policies and procedures must be implemented by the management. It is in this phase that the strategic planning process usually breaks down. Often the policies are not strong enough to be implemented properly, or are incompatible with the particular commercial bank. Or, management has no desire to implement the plans approved by the Board of Directors. There are ways management can be required to report to the Board of Directors on the implementation and efficiency of such plans (Chapter 11).

Management's Responsibility for Modifying the Strategic Plans
The professional management of the commercial bank is more attuned to the effectiveness of any implemented strategic planning policies than any other person or body politic within the organization. It is, therefore, the responsibility of management to suggest modifications, or outright elimination, of strategic planning policies. Since the management is accountable for the effectiveness of the implemented strategic plans, it is only common sense for management to be the body politic that is responsible for modifications of ineffective strategic plans.

There are no guarantees that strategic plans will work even after modification. But, professional management and the Board of Directors can only make appropriate decisions based on the information available. As time passes,

Figure 9-1   Sample Board Agenda

1. Call to order	
2. Previous board minutes	(5 minutes)
3. Financial statement review	(15 minutes)
4. Regulatory problems and analysis	(15 minutes)
5. Review of policies and decisions made at last month's meeting	(10 minutes)
6. Review of policies at regular intervals	(15 minutes)
7. Old business	(15–30 minutes)
8. Review of past due classified assets and other important items on the agenda	(15–30 minutes)
9. Loan review and approvals by board	(15–30 minutes)
10. New business	(time varies according to amount of business)
11. Questions and answers among board members	(15 minutes)
12. Free-lance board items	(15 minutes)
13. Adjournment	

and the sophistication of decision making becomes more elaborate and efficient, the modifications will become more of a fine tuning operation than a general overhaul.

Finally, don't let the directors get in and try to modify the strategic plans on their own. Either let the professional management modify the plans, under the direction of the Board of Directors, or simply get rid of the inefficient policies and/or procedures.

Management's Delegation of Strategic Planning Development Implementation to Staff

Management must delegate the job of developing specific strategic plans to staff as well as outside parties. The following steps should be taken to facilitate the orderly development of the strategic plan:

1. Receive specific strategic planning goals and objectives to be formed, i.e., the management must understand the goals.
2. Transmit specific duties and responsibilities to the staff under the senior management to develop the strategic planning process and/or its implementation.
3. Coordinate staff and senior officers in the development of the plan and reports.

4. Establish a timetable for return of materials and sub reports to the executive in charge of the planning process. This should be a timetable set in coordination with those responsible for the various sub portions of the plan, but also within the constraints set by the Board of Directors.
5. A report should be turned into the management member in charge five business days prior to the final report time.
6. All changes in the sub reports and final report to be made by the appropriate management.
7. All reports are to be submitted to the Board of Directors for their analysis three to five business days prior to the meeting.
8. All reports should be acted on by the Board or returned for additional information.

Summary

Management's role is to carry out the charges delegated by the Board of Directors. Management is accountable to the Board of Directors for the development and implementation of a strategic plan. The Board of Directors must hold management accountable for the development and implementation of the strategic plan and its overall success and efficiency as a strategic plan.

10

Microcomputers in the Planning Process

Introduction

There are numerous specific applications where a microcomputer can be used. There are nearly as many books on the market on how to use a microcomputer, as there are diet or "how to get rich" books. Therefore, don't rush into the microcomputer store (assuming you have not already been there) and purchase the cheapest package. In purchasing a microcomputer, the first time buyer should follow some basic steps. 1) Consider the application(s) for which your microcomputer will be used; 2) consider the personnel in the bank who will actually be working with it (it is critical to include them in the actual purchasing process); 3) make sure that you have an idea of the software you will need (software being all programs that run on a computer). Software, as you probably are aware, is not often interchangeable between microcomputers, therefore be very careful to select the software first. There are numerous issues that you should raise in selecting software. Listed below are some of the rules we use when looking at a specific piece of software.

1. Try to pick a product that is used all over the country. Typically, the more geographic exposure a system has, the more features it will contain.

2. Buy software only from companies that have first-hand user knowledge, as well as software design expertise. Both are very important.
3. Don't be a pioneer. Go with software that has a track record hopefully marketed by a firm with substantial personnel resources. Certainly look, ask, and receive references *and* contact them.
4. Don't select a system based on only what you think you need today. Accept the fact that your needs will change as your bank continues to grow and consider how the vendor today will be able to accommodate your requirements in the future.
5. Also be sure to check the historical pattern of the vendor's commitment to the bank's software business. You should look for consistency, growth, profitability, and a research and development investment.
6. Whenever possible, check customer references. Be very careful, however. First of all, realize that most people won't want to admit they bought a white elephant. In addition, be sure to contact references at the operating personnel level, i.e., the people who have to put up with the mistakes.

Keep in mind that there are different applications for microcomputers. Among them are word processing, data base/file management, specialized applications, graphics, and spread sheets. Make sure you clearly understand what you are going to use the microcomputer for in advance and then analyze the best software for each of these categories.

There are reams and reams of information available on how microcomputers can be used in the planning process. Some specific applications where microcomputers can be used are: 1) Analyzing the performance of your bank; 2) Analyzing your competition; 3) Gathering economic and demographic data; 4) Developing pro forma financial statements; 5) Valuation.

Analyzing the Performance of Your Bank

Do you remember when you used to have to spread a company who was looking for a loan from your bank *by hand?* Those days are long gone. Now complete software packages are written to allow the analyst to quickly and accurately determine and analyze a financial position of a potential loan candidate.

The same is true for analyzing your bank's performance. It is critical to understand where you stand at the present time in order to be able to accurately predict your future course. As a result, it is very common for the bank to use microcomputers to analyze its historical performance.

Indicated below is a thumbnail sketch of the types of information you should keep on an historical basis on your microcomputer to analyze performance of your individual bank.

1. Interest income (FTE)
2. Interest expense
3. Net interest margin
4. Trust income
5. Service charge on deposits
6. Other non-interest income
7. Salaries and benefits
8. Occupancy furniture equipment expense
9. Loan loss provision
10. Other non-interest expense
11. Less FTE adjustment
12. Tax provision
13. Return on assets—operating income
14. Return on assets—net income
15. Return on equity—net income

Yields and Rates

16. Tax equities yield-earning assets
17. Break even yield
18. Yield on investment securities (FTE)
19. Yield on loans
20. Net charge-offs % average loans
21. Loan loss provisions % average loans
22. Rate on time & savings deposits
23. Rate on total internal funds
24. Interest expense % earning assets

Capital Position

25. Effective tax rate-operating income
26. Cash dividend % operating income
27. Capital formation ratio
28. Equity capital % assets

Productivity

    29. Earning assets % assets
    30. Non-interest cash & due % assets
    31. Non-interest income % non-interest expense
    32. Personnel expense/employee
    33. Employees/million assets
    34. Non-interest income % salaries

Use of Funds
(% Earning Assets)

    35. Investment securities
    36. Federal funds sold
    37. Total loans
    38. Reserve for loan loss
    39. Real estate loans—residential
    40. Real estate loans—other
    41. Commercial & industrial loans
    42. Personal loans
    43. Agriculture/lease financing/other loans

Source of Funds
(% Earning Assets)

    44. Demand deposit IPC
    45. Public funds demand deposits
    46. Total demand deposits
    47. Savings deposits IPC
    48. Time deposits IPC
    49. Public time & savings deposits
    50. Total time & savings deposits
    51. Memo: money market CDS
    52. Memo: time deposits over 100M
    53. Foreign deposits
    54. Total deposits (foreign & domestic)
    55. Borrowings
    56. Net large liabilities
    57. Non-rate asset/liability gap

Growth Statistics

58. Income before secured transactions 1-year
59. Net income 1-year
60. Average assets 1-year
61. Income before secured transactions 5-year
62. Net income 5-year
63. Average assets 5-year

This type of information is readily available on your bank through a number of services. Perhaps the most efficient way to gather this information is to utilize an on-line service such as Innerline. For a small fee this type of information can be quickly and accurately received by using a microcomputer with a modem. In addition, this type of information can be gathered on your competition to see how you have fared on a historical basis versus your local and not so local commercial bank competition.

Analyzing Competition

Certainly a key part of your master plan is to monitor what's happening in your environment and what your competition is doing locally. This type of information can be easily obtained on any other competition without them knowing it. Part of the beauty of this type of analysis is the confidentiality.

In addition, you should keep market data on key accounts such as assets, loans, and deposits for your general trade area. So it may be the microcomputer is an excellent place to start.

Economic and Demographic Data

An important part of any master plan is to factor in the type of economic environment in which the organization will operate. A microcomputer can assist you in this task by using a number of services which are available over a modem. Executive Information Service offered by Compuserve (a division by H&R Block) will give you the following information for any area over a microcomputer using a modem. This information can be broken down by country, city, state, or even on a detailed basis as a zip code.

Demographic Analysis

1. Historic, current, and projected demographic and income data
2. Data broken down by U.S., state, county, and zip code

3. Sales potential for 16 major types of retail stores
4. Sales potential for 74 merchandise lines
5. Consumer potential for three types of financial institutions
6. Total potential for three types of financial institutions
7. Family and household income by race
8. Average, median, and per capita income
9. Sources of household income
10. Home values, condominium prices, and rental prices
11. Units in structure, including year structure built
12. Industrial and occupational breakdown
13. Automobile and utilities
14. Achieved education level of adults by race
15. Current educational level enrollment by race
16. Household and family composition
17. Major household appliances
18. Energy usage patterns
19. Transportation and travel time to work
20. Labor force by race and age
21. Unemployment by race

Economic Analysis

1. Population trends
2. Housing unit trends
3. Total labor force
4. Unemployment rates
5. Labor force characteristics
6. Major employers within county
7. Median family income
8. Median household effective buying income
9. Percent of households with income in excess of $15,000
10. Percent of households by effective buying income group
11. Retail sales
12. Other (agricultural/travel/tourism statistics)
13. Financial institutions located within the county
14. Deposit growth
15. Deposit market share

By developing this type of information on a microcomputer, it can constantly be updated to reflect changing demographic and economic trends. In addition, this type of information will give you and your management a better idea of the type of economic environment you currently compete in and trends that may affect an overall long-term game plan.

Pro Forma Financial Statements

Certainly one of the most important uses of a microcomputer in the planning process is to develop pro forma financial statements. Part of the deal of using a microcomputer for this task is that as assumptions and other factors change balance sheets and income statements for the future can alter to accurately reflect these critical assumptions. There are numerous programs that can be purchased by you to assist you in this task.

Valuation

Certainly one of the more important uses of a microcomputer is the valuation process. The reason to use a microcomputer here is similar to why you should use one in reference to pro forma financial statements; as assumptions change on a target bank, or even your bank, changes can be made to accurately reflect these changes. It is important to keep in mind that there are really two types of valuations which can be used in reference to a master plan: valuation of your bank and valuation of a potential target. In either case, there is software available which will allow the analyst to quickly and accurately factor in a large number of assumptions to determine what a potential bank is worth.

Summary

There are numerous spots in your game plan where a microcomputer can be used. Indicated above are just a couple of the more important ones. As significant as the different areas where a microcomputer can be used are the types of software available and sources of information where you can find help.

Exhibit A   Where to Get More Information

I. *Books*
   1. Micros in Banking
      M. Arthur Gillis
      Computer Based Solutions, Inc.
      3390 Peachtree Road N.E.
      Suite 1148
      Atlanta, Georgia 30326
      (404) 261-0501

II. *Newsletters*
   1. Microbanker
      Robert H. Long, Editor
      P.O. Box 95193
      Schaumburg, Illinois 60195
      (312) 397-0970
   2. Micro Banking Report
      John J. Jedlicka, Editor
      P.O. Box 88913
      Atlanta, Georgia 30356
      (404) 396-6795

III. *Directories, Reports and Monographs*
   1. Microbanker Software Directory
      P.O. Box 1508
      York, Pennsylvania 17405
      (717) 848-4782
   2. BAI—Bank Microcomputers, 1983
      60 Gould Center
      Rolling Meadows, Illinois 60008
      (312) 228-6200   (800) 323-8552
   3. Bank Systems and Equipment
      Buyers' Guide 1984
      1515 Broadway
      New York, New York 10036
      (212) 869-1300
   4. International Computer Programs (Software Directory)
      P.O. Box 40946
      Indianapolis, Indiana 46240
      (317) 844-7461   (800) 428-6179

5. Datapro Reports on Microcomputers
   Datapro Research Corporation
   1805 Underwood Boulevard
   Delran, New Jersey 08075
   (609) 764-0100   (800) 257-9406
6. Funds Management Software Resource Directory
   American Bankers Association
   1120 Connecticut Avenue, N.W.
   Washington, D.C. 20036
   (202) 467-4000
7. BAI Books:
   • Acquisition Guidelines for Small Computer Systems
   • Security, Audit and Control for Small Computer Systems
   • Bank Data Security Bulletins
8. American Bankers Association:
   Community Bank Financial Performance Guide
   Micro Modeling
9. In-House Computer Survey for Community Banks
   Computer Based Solutions, Inc.
   3390 Peachtree Road N.E.
   Suite 1148
   Atlanta, Georgia 30326
   (404) 261-0501

IV. *Magazines*
   1. Bank Systems and Equipment, 1515 Broadway, New York, New
      York 10036 (212) 869-1300
   2. Computers in Banking (New), Faulkner Communications Co., 870
      Seventh Avenue, Suite 31-E, New York, New York 10019 (212)
      247-1690
   3. Financial Computing (New), Cleworth Publishing Co., Inc., One
      River Road, Cos Cob, Connecticut 06807 (203) 661-5000
   4. PC Magazine, One Park Avenue, New York, NY 10016
   5. PC World, 555 De Huro St., San Francisco, CA 94107
   6. Absolute Reference (The Journal for 1-2-3® users), 7999 Kane
      Road, Indianapolis, IN 46250

V. *Banking Publications*
   ABA Banking Journal, P.O. Box 530, Bristol, CT 06010, 1 yr. $20
   (Monthly)
   American Banker, One State Street Plaza, New York, NY 10004, 1 yr.
   $395 (Daily)
   The Magazine of Bank Administration, 60 Gould Center, Rolling Mead-
   ows, IL 60008, $30 yr. (Monthly)

Washington Financial Reports, The Bureau of National Affairs, Inc., 1231 25th St., Washington, D.C. 20037, 1 yr. $970 (every Monday, except Labor Day and the Monday following Christmas)

Bankers Monthly, 601 Skokie Blvd., Northbrook, IL 60062, 1 yr. $18 (Monthly)

VI. *Banking Publications*

United States Banker, One River Road, Cos Cob, CT 06807, 1 yr. $21 (Monthly)

Mid-Continent Banker, 408 Olive, St. Louis, MO 63102, 1 yr $12 (Monthly)

Journal of Bank Research (published by BAI) 60 Gould Center, Rolling Meadows, IL 60008, 1 yr. $30 (Quarterly)

Microcomputer Publications

PC Magazine, One Park Avenue, New York, NY 10016, 1 yr. $34.97 (Bi-weekly)

PC World, 555 De Huro St., San Francisco, CA 94107, 1 yr. $24 (Monthly except semi-monthly in June and December)

Absolute Reference (The Journal for 1-2-3® users), 7999 Kane Road, Indianapolis, IN 46250, 1 yr. $60 (Monthly)

VII. *General Business Publications*

Cashflow, 1807 Glenview Road, Glenview, IL 60025, 1 yr. $50 (10 issues a year, monthly except combined issues January/February and July/August)

Barron's (Monday) 200 Burnett Road, Chicopee, Mass. 01021, 1 yr. $71.

The Wall Street Journal, 200 Burnett Road, Chicopee, Mass. 01021, 1 yr. $107.

Fortune, 3435 Wilshire Blvd., Los Angeles, CA 90010, 1 yr. $39

VIII. *Regulator/Regulation Publications*

Economic Review, Research Division, Federal Reserve Bank of Kansas City, 925 Grand Avenue, Kansas City, MO 64198 (Free)

Review, Research and Public Information Department of the Federal Reserve Bank of St. Louis, P.O. Box 442, St. Louis, MO 63166 (Free)

Economic Review Information Center, Federal Reserve Bank of Atlanta, P.O. Box 1731, Altanta, GA 30301 (Free)

Economic Perspectives Information Center, Federal Reserve Bank of Chicago, P.O. Box 834, Chicago, IL 60690 (Free)

Issues in Bank Regulation (published by BAI), 60 Gould Center, Rolling Meadows, IL 60008, 1 yr. $28 (Quarterly)

IX. *State Magazines*

The Ohio Banker (Monthly)

The Ohio Community Banker (Monthly)
The Michigan Investor (Weekly)
The Hoosier Banker (Monthly)

X. *Training Aids*
American Bankers Association:
1. Videotape of Microcomputers Seminar
2. Decision Support Training Program using Lotus 1-2-3 (A tutorial diskette and manual)

XI. *Conferences, Seminars and Workshops*
  1. Microscope
     BAI
     October 30–November 2, 1984
     Dallas, Texas

  2. BAI Microcomputer Workshops
     Five scheduled in 1984
  3. ABA
     National Operations and Automation Conference
     May 13–15, 1984
     Washington, D.C.
  4. ABA
     Micro Training Centers
     Nine AIB Chapters

XII. *Co-sponsored Research Study*
Electronic Banking, Inc.
American Banker
3420 Norman Berry Drive
Suite 623
Atlanta, Georgia 30354
(404) 768-3964

Exhibit B   Specific Software Applications for Use of the Microcomputer

1. Administrative applications
   A. Asset liability and management forecasting
   B. Asset liability and management planning
   C. Asset liability and management hedging
   D. Financial analysis
   E. Call reports
   F. Financial reporting and board reports
   G. Executive work station
2. Credit applications
   A. Accounting programs
      a. general accounting
      b. accounting for commercial loans
      c. central information files
   B. Analysis programs
      a. credit analysis
3. Loan processing programs
   A. Credit calculations
   B. Commercial loan processing
   C. Installment loan processing
   D. Mortgage loan processing
   E. Credit bureau access
4. Loan loss control
5. Agriculture applications
   A. Analysis
   B. General ledger
   C. Management
6. Operations applications
   A. Accounting programs
      a. accounts receivable
      b. central information file
      c. credit card operations
      d. deposit accounting
      e. escrow accounting
      f. fixed asset accounting
      g. federal funds accounting
      h. funds transfer accounting
      i. general accounting
      j. general ledger accounting
      k. lease accounting
      l. retirement accounting

7. Security accounting
   A. Investment security accounting
   B. Certificate of deposit accounting
   C. Repurchase agreement accounting
   D. Sweep accounting
8. Analysis programs
   A. Cost accounting analysis
   B. Currency analysis & control
   C. Float analysis & control
   D. Lease purchase analysis
9. Calculation programs
10. Computer operation programs
11. Customer service programs
   A. Certificates of deposit sales & service
   B. Check reconciliation and cross selling general
   C. Home banking
   D. IRA/KEOGH sales & service
   E. Mortgage sales & service
   F. General operations applications
   G. Miscellaneous applications
12. Marketing programs
13. Night deposit processing
14. Personnel programs
   A. Payroll
   B. Record keeping & training
15. Performance evaluation programs
16. Purchasing programs
17. Reporting programs
18. Safe deposit operations
19. Investment applications
   A. Accounting programs
      a. bond accounting
      b. employee stock option plan accounting
      c. general ledger accounting
      d. hedge accounting
      e. pension/profit sharing plan accounting
      f. stockholder/shareholder accounting
      g. trust accounting
20. Analysis programs
   A. Security investment analysis
   B. Public debt analysis & planning
21. Calculation programs
22. Maintenance

23. Marketing
24. Processing programs
    A. Security processing
    B. Trust accounting processing
25. Safe keeping programs

Microbanker has published a five volume (4 separate books plus a supplement) set indicating different types of software available for use on a microcomputer for banks. The directories list approximately 700 financial microcomputer programs from over 200 vendors. The most recent addition of this software directory had three times the number listed in the first directory, first put out in 1982. Microbanker can be contacted for more information at P.O. Box 1508, York, Pennsylvania 17405 or by calling (717) 848-4782.

Exhibit C   Specific Applications of Microcomputers

These are excellent examples of the different types of specific applications where microcomputers have been used in banks. These were originally presented in *The American Banker* and are summarized below.

A. Teller machine cost monitored. ATM cost model which allows a holding company to know existing or anticipated costs of ATM facilities. Costs are expressed in terms of total cost, cost per teller machine, and cost per transaction. Installation costs include capital expenditure for the ATM hardware and installation, site preparation, ATM facility, external lighting, landscaping, currency cartridges, camera, and alarms. Operating costs include other expenditures for communications, supplies, data processing, after-hour servicing, hardware maintenance, back office costs, electricity, currency replenishment, janitorial services, site lease, access cards, and charge-off losses. Output is broken down according to the type of facility. Therefore, costs can be shown for both off-premise ATMs and on-premise ATMs, utilizing Lotus 1-2-3 (Virginia BHC).

B. Getting a handle on resumes. The Personnel Department of bank implements an efficient resume tracking system using an IBM-PC. Previously, resumes received were handled by respective personnel counsellors. Problems occurred based on the fact that 10,000 resumes were received annually. The IBM has all but eliminated problems in resume tracking. When a resume is received, it is entered into the hard disc of the IBM-PC, with uniformity in all entries. For each resume entry, counsellor initials applicant's name, date received, source (i.e., add response referral, walk-in, agency, etc.), and the position applied for. After resume has been received and an outcome decided, the results are entered into the computer (Wisconsin bank).

C. Keeping personnel records. Using microcomputer technology to streamline the personnel record-keeping task. Before microcomputer was on line, personnel information was reviewed during lengthy management meetings. With so much information on the table at one time, it was often difficult to conceptualize overall strategy. Now that microcomputer is fed information which is categorized in accord with various criteria agreed to by the staff, the microcomputer makes it far easier to see how all the pieces comprise a bigger picture and a great deal of time is saved. A typical managers' meeting has been cut from half-day to half-hour or 45-minute sessions. The productivity level is much higher (California bank).

D. Verification speeded. Until recently, test code verification process between departments, branches and funds transfer department was costly and time-consuming. An Apple II computer solved these problems and reduced the chances of error. Test code verification involves interlocking codes with which a bank electronically gives to another bank holding its account the equivalent of an authorized signature to credit or debit that account. Previously, the test code verification process required several minutes to complete. Each verification was done manually. We had to assign two members of the staff to oversee the process. Because of security, neither was assigned to other related tasks. The new system can perform the entire function in a fraction of the time the previous application took. Since it is protected by the use of functional passwords, we do not have to assign full-time personnel to oversee its use. Because we are now utilizing the computer system, we are able to verify tests in 75 percent less time than the previous manual system required (New Jersey bank).

E. Customer charge application. Calculating monthly charges for customers was once a 35-hour per month task. To expedite the process, the cash management department purchased an IBM-XT and Lotus 1-2-3. The bottom line—after running effectively for more than two months, this application has reduced execution time to 10 hours a month, a saving of 25 hours over the previous system (Minnesota bank).

F. Evaluating a loan request. A microcomputer was used to evaluate an unusual real estate loan request. The prospective borrower arrived with a detailed three-year projection of the transaction which he had done laboriously on paper. As one might expect, the detail was a successful and profitable venture for him and indicated a timely and orderly repayment of the loan. But there were many more variables to consider. The most important were interest rates and projected sale prices of the cooperative apartments my customer planned to market. What effect would changes in these variables have on the projected repayment of the loan? To answer these questions would have required duplication—several times over—what obviously had taken my potential borrower many hours of work. The loan officer simply reproduced this work just once, using a spread sheet program on a microcomputer. Several alternative cases were then tried using the bank's expectation of market conditions. The rate calculation took literally only seconds and allowed the loan officer to spend time on the true business aspects of the proposal. Without the microcomputer, the tools would have been a pencil, paper, and calculator, and a five-fold increase in the time to complete the mathematics (New York bank).

G. Time sharing supplemented. The Trust Division at our bank uses a time-sharing system as its primary trust accounting system. In order to provide customized services and reports, this system is supplemented by an in-house microcomputer. The system has dramatically enhanced the productivity of the bank's staff by reducing data entry time and providing data entry screens which make sense to the user because the users had developed the screens. Another benefit of the system is that it has stirred enthusiasm in the use of microcomputers within our division more than any other single application [Spread sheet, graph plotting, word processing, etc.] (Pennsylvania bank).

H. Answering branch inquiries. At this bank, an internal task force has been actively working since January to develop an outstanding microcomputer system for the branch network. Designed to inform customers about bank products and assist staff in preparing forms and answering questions, the IBM-XTs are scheduled for implementation in July, 1984. The use of microcomputers by branch management and customer service representatives will provide quick, personalized service to customers in various ways. The products screen or menu will feature personalized product descriptions for each of our bank's services. With product information at such easy access representatives will quickly and easily present customers with product options (Kentucky bank).

I. Close watch on outside balances. Timely cash management decisions are critical for any corporation and many large businesses utilize the cash management information system provided by their bank to maintain close watch on their balances. Banks, too, are faced with the same critical information need if they are to effectively manage their own balances with other banks. At this bank, the cash position division supported by our systems group is responsible for the maintenance of target balance levels in various demand deposit accounts maintained with other banks throughout the country. In order to monitor accounts with other banks, we developed a system for cash positions that automatically retrieves credit information from the balance reporting systems of other banks using microcomputers. This program utilizes Lotus 1-2-3 spread sheets. The systems group currently is monitoring the cash position pilot projects and expects to discover personnel savings as well as improvements in the timing and quality of cash management (Chicago bank).

J. Sending banker's acceptances. In late 1982, this Dallas bank opened an Edge Act corporation in New York City. One of the services that it wished to offer to its head office was the ability for them to deliver our banker's acceptances from Dallas to our office in New York, but a twofold problem occurred. (1) How to get physical drafts from Dallas to New York on the same day of creation, or (2) how could it be sure of creating the acceptance without the inevitable transmission errors. The solution: give Dallas a microcomputer with an entry screen to fill out, and then transmit the acceptance form to New York. The resultant banker's acceptance can sometimes be created within 45 minutes of leaving the lender's office hands in Dallas (Dallas bank).

K. Asset/liability process. The use of the microcomputer in the corporate finance department has made our asset and liability management process more flexible and accurate. Before the micro, our asset and liability management models available from a large computer to a time-sharing arrangement, the transmission of data was slow and cumbersome, and the service was costly. As a result, we didn't utilize our models as we should have. The micro gave us easy access to our forecasting models and allowed us the flexibility to develop our own in-house modeling capability (North Carolina bank).

L. Resolving complaints. The increase in the number and complexity of consumer complaints confronting the bank in the past few years necessitated a systematic way of tracking the receipt, internalization of resolution of such complaints in order to comply with institutional and regulatory guidelines. Through the use of a microcomputer, the bank has cut down the paper work and increased the effectiveness of dealing with consumer complaints. All complaints, whether they emanate from regulatory agencies or individual customers, are inputted into the computer. They are coded by categories—Reg. E., employee behavior, policy complaint, etc. They are also coded by branch and region within the bank. No names of either customer or employee are inputted because the system is not to be viewed as an audit for Big Brother watching over the proceedings. Computer tracking of complaints provides for centralized source of information, for providing the bank's management with reports of trends and remedies for complaints (California bank).

M. Corporate planning and research. This bank purchased its first microcomputer almost four years ago for use in its corporate planning and research department. Today, the bank uses micros in numerous departments to handle word processing, data base, storage graphics, and spread sheet analysis of the institution's competitive positioning. Asset and liability models and merger and acquisition analysis are also major ongoing projects using the micro. The corporate planning and research department found that it could gain flexibility and lower costs by purchasing its own microcomputers. One of the first applications developed for the micro in the corporate planning and research department was a merger and acquisition modeling analysis. The model quotes historical data on the bank and also contains projections of bank performance and growth over several years. For each merger prospect, its financial history is loaded, pro forma projections are analyzed, and various merger scenarios are constructed (Mississippi bank).

N. At this bank, they are currently using a software system to determine customer profitability. After defining the "total customer" by all business and personal accounts and relationships, the pertinent data—balance and interest rate, service charges and income and fees and expenses are fed into the system along with calculation for the bank's standard or expected yields. The result of this input is a printout showing balances provided or used, income expense and profit or loss for each banking application. The bottom line shows the total customer income expense, profit or loss. The calculations for the bank's standard give each customer a rating which is again calculated against the index (Arizona bank).

O. Quick portfolio analysis. Two years ago the Senior Vice President and Chief Investment Officer of this bank recognized the need for staff to make decisions based on up-to-the-minute financial information. This bank's trust and investment department got microcomputers, and today they have 30 microcomputers to provide solutions to problems by combining communications and data management software. Each micro can access the trust accounting system, store and manipulate data, and transfer data between micro disk and mainframe, thereby eliminating many more expensive specialized terminals. They were limited to task specific functions (Pennsylvania bank).

P.   Tracking funds at other banks. In 1982, the head of this bank's investment division approached the information and operations services division with a problem and a request. In order to keep track of the bank's balances with other banks, primarily the New York staff members and bank investment, the bank was using manual spread sheets, which were large, unwieldy charts requiring the entry efforts and supervision of a full-time balance manager. After gaining and giving information from several bank departments over the phone and maintaining that information on a number of additional machine tapes, the clerk would enter those numbers on a sheet, sometimes even using different colors of ink for different classes of transactions. Another person would double-check the entries during several balancing cutoffs. If they didn't balance as many as 100 figures, 100 figures might have to be rechecked before the error was found. This was obviously a tedious and time-consuming process. It took just 11 days to design and install the system using a microcomputer. Today the microcomputer performs all calculations accurately, writes summary instructions to a wire transfer area on what funds the bank needs to send out or should expect to come in, and allows us to assess our net position at any time instead of waiting up to 25 or 30 minutes after reaching our cutoff to balance. At the final cutoff of the report, the microcomputer automatically provides a complete report summarizing all transactions. The total cost? About $5,000 (Michigan bank).

11

Accountability and Review

Implementation, Modification, and Review

Strategic planning simply doesn't work only because it is thought out, mapped out, and approved by the Board of Directors. It must be implemented, modified where necessary, and reviewed on a regular basis. This chapter helps you to implement your strategic planning, modify it when the flags and bells tell you its not working, and review it on a regular basis.

Importance of Proper Implementation

Up to this point strategic planning has been stressed. We've examined how to set goals and objectives; how to reach the strategic planning objectives; and how to focus on the proper quantitative and qualitative mix. However, at this stage, assuming that the decision has been made to go forth with certain short-term and long-term strategic planning policies, it is time to implement them. Improper implementation of the policies reached by the Board of Directors is as bad as no policies at all.

Appropriate delegation is the key. The Board of Directors are not implements. The management and the staff of the commercial bank are the implements of the strategic plan and its components. Therefore, the delegation of appropriate management and/or staff members is the key to the first phase of implementation.

The second aspect of proper implementation is the clarification and understanding of the management and staff of the strategic policies to be followed. To put this another way, if you received the directive, could you understand it and follow it? The Board of Directors should make sure that management and staff know clearly and succinctly what they are supposed to implement and what results are to be obtained. For example, it is undoubtedly easier to implement the fiscal budget for year 198X than it is to report back to the Board of Directors on the performance of the 198X affirmative action program. On the other hand, both must be reported back to the Board of Directors after successful implementation in order for the plan to work.

Another key to proper implementation is to make sure that all of the strategic plans and policies are implemented. It has not been unusual in some cases for management against certain policies to refuse to implement such policies. Since the Board of Directors often never asked how the policy was going, or what the procedure was, the management simply never did anything and the Board of Directors never knew any better. Thus, one important ingredient of good implementation is to make sure implementation takes place in the first place. And, the proper communication back to the Board of Directors is essential for such proper implementation.

Accountability

Accountability has been noted previously under implementation. Accountability sounds terrible—it actually means that some of your people are responsible for their actions. Accountability works both ways—excellent performance should be rewarded, and subpar performance should be punished, even to the degree of removal.

Your strategic plans and their tangible output will be more likely to succeed if your staff and management knows it can be held accountable for such policies. This does not mean that they have to act as robots simply implementing all decisions without comment, input, or modification. But if everyone knows that they are being held accountable for all of their actions, including senior management, the chances are your implementation results will be improved.

Modification

Any commercial bank that implements strategic plans and does not anticipate any modification is asking for serious trouble. An integral part of the implementation and review of your strategic planning process is the modification of policies, procedures, and plans which simply aren't working. Just because they're not working doesn't mean that they can't be modified and improved. However, there may be several decisions that will have to be reversed simply because the policy wasn't any good in the first place. Since the worst decision is no decision, correction of a bad decision is not a fatal flaw in the management and/or direction of the bank. Needless to say, you shouldn't have to reverse all your decisions because of incompetency. The quick reversal of bad decisions will not significantly impact the bank's ability to serve the community and to be a profitable institution.

Regular Review
Modification cannot take place without regular review. Review of the strategic planning, policies, procedures, and plans is an essential key to the efficient operation of your bank. We find that not only do the Board of Directors of the commercial banks not know whether their policies procedures and/or decisions have been implemented, they fail to do so by neglecting to review their decisions on a periodic basis. This can have disastrous consequences, unless the management is so competent that it covers up for the incompetency of the Board of Directors. On the other hand, the management may be so incompetent, and devious, that they don't want to report the results back to the Board of Directors and do not. Thus, in order to be able to protect the shareholders, let us outline some ways by which the regular review can take place and by which decisions can be made by the Board of Directors.

Figure 11-1 is a decision matrix which your Board of Directors can use for determination of regular review of your decisions. It's not a complicated device—but it works. If you don't have such a decision matrix agenda, decisions can get lost and you'll never know whether they've been implemented or not.

There is no magic to how review takes place. Every commercial bank could use a different technique. This technique is illustrative, but also functional. So, you might wish to adopt it or a modification.

The person who should be responsible for this decision matrix (review agenda) is the secretary of the Board of Directors. That's the person who is responsible for all the board minutes, and answers to the Chairman of the Board at the meetings (The Chairman of the Board, remember, is the person responsible to the shareholders for the proper functioning of the bank and is the chairperson of the Board of Directors). The secretary should handle all of these matters, and coordinate between the management and the Board of Directors concerning the review of all policies.

Figure 11-1   Decision Review Format

Decision	Frequency of review Monthly/Quarterly Semi-annually Annually	Review decision taken	Responsible party
(Illustrations)			
1. 198X budget			
2. Management recruiting			
3. Merit raises			
4. Additional fringe benefits			
5. Administrative agency memorandum			
6. Capital adequacy problems			

All decisions of the Board of Directors should be reviewed. The only difference is how regularly they should be reviewed, and in how much depth. The Board of Directors will never know whether their actions have been implemented, including strategic planning decisions, unless they are reviewed on a regular basis. Thus the review format is essential to the proper implementation and review of the strategic planning policies and procedures of your bank.

Figure 11-1 indicates that the review format can be relatively simple. All you need to note are the decisions that need to be reviewed, and the degree of frequency of such review. Not all decisions need to be reviewed each month, and some are not even capable of having enough transpired events to justify monthly review. These could be reviewed every two months, every quarter, or whatever is appropriate. This is the type of decision that should be made by the Board of Directors and the management at the time the decision is reached, i.e., the date of the review. The next important item to note is the decision reached at the time of review and to note on the format itself the de-

Figure 11-2   Hypothetical National Bank Board Meeting October 30, 198X Agenda

1. Call to order
2. Secretary's minutes
3. Monthly financial report
4. Review of past decisions—scheduled decisions on yearly calendar:
   a. Decisions brought to board by management and/or directors of interest
5. Report of bank examiners
6. Loan committee recommendations for approval of new loans
7. Review of loans approved by delegated authority
8. Report of classified assets
9. Old business
10. New business
11. Adjournment

cision made by the board after a review. This would not only include the modifications necessary, but also a notation if the Board of Directors felt that a different review schedule was necessary. Finally, the format requires that the appropriate responsible party must be noted. This party does not have to be a member of the Board of Directors. Nor should it automatically be president and chief executive officer. Each of the types of decisions reached by the Board of Directors and implemented by management may have a different responsible party. The person responsible is the one that should report and review the decision and the implementation of the decision plan or procedure with the Board of Directors. That person could be an assistant vice president, a chief executive officer, or anyone in between. The Board of Directors may get to know more about their staff and management through this type of accountability system than they will simply through the recommendations of senior management.

Decision Review on the Board's Agenda

Each commercial bank should have this type of board decision review on its agenda. It should become as much a part of the agenda as the secretary's minutes or the financial report. This permits the directors to reflect on the decisions that have been made over the last months or years and to determine whether the decisions were appropriate or not. Modifications can be made based upon the totality of the decision review, since it is very likely that the board members will forget what decisions have been made and what the expected results were from previous decisions. If this type of review is done on a regular basis, the board can keep an overall idea of how the commercial bank is progressing, and how the strategic planning decisions, and other decisions are impacting the staff, management, and the public served by the bank.

Figure 11-2 is a typical Board of Directors' agenda for a mythical commercial bank showing the decision review format thrown into the normal agenda. The decision review each month does not have to be lengthy. The time it takes will vary depending on what decisions were made at the meeting. Reports concerning the review and the accountability of the decision should be attached to the board agenda and the responsible party brought in to discuss the matter involved. At the end of the review, the board should decide what to do concerning the matter for its next review, and excuse the responsible party and continue with the board meeting.

Deal with the legitimate job of appraising what is going wrong with the decisions you have made and make adjustments or refinements. Just because something hasn't worked out precisely as you wanted—don't discard the entire proposition. Use as much time and effort to determine how to modify the decision as you did in judging whether to discard the original decision. Research and analyze again. If you do this, the modifications you make will be in line with the improvement of your planning process.

Summary

Implementing your strategic planning decisions is not easy. It takes constructive objective planning. Once the decisions have been reached, the implementation phase must take place. Implementation must be handled by the appropriate delegated management and/or staff members, and must be delegated to them by the appropriate board members. In addition, modification of previous decisions should be analyzed based upon the efficiency of the decisions. Accountability and review are essential for the successful completion of your strategic planning process. Regular review at the board level utilizing the board meetings themselves is essential for the overall effectiveness of the bank. If the Board of Directors does not demand review of decisions and the implementation of such decisions in concrete planning, how can the board realize whether such plans have ever been implemented and how effective they are. Alternatively, if the board doesn't demand review, decisions often will not be implemented, or if implemented will not bring the desired results. Therefore, overall review of the implementation is essential to the success of the strategic plan. It would be a shame if all the time and effort spent in developing a strategic plan went down the drain because the Board of Directors forgot to hold the management and staff accountable for the implementation of the strategic planning process. Or, the board was too incompetent to review the implementation and effectiveness of their own plans as a check and balance to the overall process.

12

Situation Analysis

We want to review the specific technique for analyzing strengths and weaknesses. We call it "The Situation Analysis," and we use it in our business to assist our clients in determining the strengths and weaknesses of their operations. It is good not only for commercial banks, but for any business, whether it be a bank, savings and loan association, industrial corporation, or a non-profit organization. The Situation Analysis is first used to assist the Board of Directors and management to determine the strengths and weaknesses of the business in order to assist in overall long-term strategic planning for the business. All of the aspects of strategic planning that we have outlined for community banks in the previous eleven chapters are important. But, a self-analysis is crucial to assist in determining strengths and weaknesses in order to provide the appropriate direction for your bank. Therefore, we recommend that you use a form of this situation analysis to determine your strengths and weaknesses in order to prepare yourself for the long-term and short-term strategic planning necessary for corporate survival.

In the pages that follow, we shall outline how the situation analysis operates, how it can apply to your own situation, and what kinds of results you can expect. With the situation analysis behind you, it will assist you in determining

Figure 12-1   Situation Analysis Questions

Describe *general effectiveness* of the function area
    Level of service to customers
    Level of service to internal bank areas/people
    Does it actively solicit new business
Describe effectiveness of *communication* of the functional area
    Written reports
    Oral reports
    Informal communication
    Communication to right people
Describe effectiveness of the *organization* of the functional area
    Proper staff level
    Efficiently organized
    Expertise of support staff—properly trained
    Leadership of manager
    Recommended changes to improve
Describe the area's *contribution to bank profits*
    Strive to control expenses
    Maximize income
Describe the area's *ability to plan for the future*
    Does it have growth potential
    Does it anticipate and plan for growth
        People
        Systems
    Does it anticipate and plan for operating problems
    Do problems become crises
    Do people have the expertise
    Does it anticipate and plan for industry changes
    Knowledge of industry changes
    Planning and discussion of possible changes
Describe the area's understanding of bank's *goals and objectives*
    Participation in budgeting
    Participation in planning
    Operation of department in concert with rest of organization

short term and long term strategic planning necessary for your commercial bank to succeed.

The first step in a situation analysis is to review the organizational chart and the job descriptions of your bank. Many commercial banks do not have current job descriptions nor do they have an organizational chart that depicts the functional organization of that business. This means that the first step is to analyze job descriptions and to compile accurate job descriptions of the staff and management of your bank. *Job Descriptions in Banking* published by

Bankers Publishing Company would be helpful. Furthermore, an organizational chart of exactly what is taking place today should be developed. This may not be the organizational chart that you thought you had, nor the organizational chart you want, but it is the first step in determining your current situation.

The next phase of the situation analysis is to develop a series of questions which will be used in interviewing members of the Board of Directors, senior management, and selected staff members to determine the current weaknesses and strengths of your organization. These questions must be tailor made to your individual institution and are for purposes of drawing from the interviewees the strengths and weaknesses of the organization, as well as the objectives and goals of the organization. It should result in an appraisal of the current position of the bank. Figure 12-1 is an illustrative set of questions used by us in previous situation analyses. But these questions are illustrative only. Do not consider them to be relevant for your own personal situation. They are simply illustrative of the areas that should be covered in developing questions to better analyze the strengths and weaknesses of your bank.

There are several areas to be covered by the interviews and they are extremely important to the evaluation of the current position of the bank. They are the bank's public image, the expertise of the functional areas of the bank, the strengths and weaknesses of the management and staff, the direction of the Board of Directors, the goals and objectives of the institution, the marketing and advertising effectiveness of the bank, and the leadership of senior management and the Board of Directors. Interviews are also used to determine the communication efficiency among staff members of the bank and the degree of communication between management and the Board of Directors. In addition, analysis should be made of the committee structure within management and the Board of Directors and its perceived degree of efficiency. Finally, this interview process will also determine management's and the Board of Directors' perception of the prospects for successful operation in the future and any financial aspects of the bank which will promote or deter from profitable operations.

After the development of the interview questionnaires, interviews should take place in a confidential manner. This is by far the most difficult stage of the situation analysis. You may wish to have such interviews done by an outside consulting group in order to promote confidentiality and yet at the same time encourage full disclosure by the interviewees. The interviews are designed to emphasize the functional areas of the organization, and to probe for weaknesses and strengths of the organization. They should not center on personalities and/or individuals. However, such personal individual situations do arise as a part of the interview process so it is best to use outside objective consultants to assist you in this stage of the analysis to permit the best informational flow at the least possible political cost. Every effort should be made to keep office politics and personal conflicts out of the interview and/or situation analysis process. All interviewees should be informed that any comments or criticisms shall not be in the report under any individual's name. All strength and weakness recommendations and the recommendations of the situation analysis are a consensus of the interviewees and do not originate (point directly) from any single individual interviewed concerning their opinions. This is done to protect the interviewees, but at the same time to get to the strengths and weaknesses of the institution, so that the right recommendations are made in order to improve the bank.

By ensuring confidentiality, each individual interviewee is prompted to objectively disclose the strengths and weaknesses of his or her own functional area and to analyze the strengths and weaknesses of the entire institution. As the interview consensus forms, the apparent and latent strengths and weaknesses of the commercial bank appear to the interviewers. Then they can be transmitted to the Board of Directors and senior management through the situation analysis report and recommendations.

It should be noted that the efficiency or inefficiency of each individual department head, supervisor, or officer of the bank will be a bi-product of the situation analysis. Not only will the individuals in charge of functional areas respond to their own weaknesses or strengths but, at the same time, on the strengths and weaknesses on the other department heads and senior management, as well as members of the Board of Directors. The purpose of this cross fertilization concerning efficiency of management is to give senior management and the Board of Directors an objective appraisal of the strengths and weaknesses of the bank itself, and to assist in determining where weaknesses must be remedied through increased training, new individuals, or deletion of individuals who are not responsible or efficient.

The final phase of the situation analysis is the report itself. The report, either prepared internally or on a consulting basis, brings forth a consensus of the positive and negative aspects of the commercial bank. Then it makes recommendations relating to the improvement of the weakest areas and assists in assessing the meritorious conduct of certain functional areas and individuals.

This report is designed to assist the Board of Directors and the senior management, as a part of the overall strategic planning process, to analyze the current strengths and weaknesses of the bank, and to understand what types of changes must be made in order to improve the bank's overall operation. In addition to increasing the strengths of various operational departments, changing

Figure 12-2   Situation Analysis Report

ABC National Bank

   I. Executive Summary
  II. Introduction
 III. Methodology
     A. Review of financial information
     B. Interview questionnaires
     C. Interview process
     D. Other materials
  IV. Perception of public image
     A. Management and Board of Directors
     B. Staff
     C. Customers
     D. Shareholders
     E. Public
   V. Comparison of bank with bank and depository institution competitors
  VI. Marketing and Advertising Appraisal
     A. Advertising comparisons
     B. Marketing efforts
     C. Market research
     D. Perception by public
 VII. Functional areas of the bank appraised
     A. Lending
        1. commercial and industrial lending
        2. installment lending
        3. mortgage lending
        4. other lending activities
        5. compliance
        6. collections
        7. branch lending
        8. credit analysis and review
     B. Deposit taking activities
        1. operations
        2. customer oriented services
     C. Trust department
        1. operations

Figure 12-2   (*continued*)

      2. customer solicitation
      3. administration
   D. Personnel
   E. Branch administration
   F. Bank operations
   G. Senior management
   H. Board of Directors
   I. Accounting
   J. Auditing
   K. Special services, such as discount brokerage
   L. Committee structure and effectiveness
VIII. Strengths of bank, rank by priority
  IX. Weaknesses of bank, rank by priority
   X. Communication strengths and weaknesses
  XI. Recommendations—explicit and specific
 XII. Conclusions

functional characteristics of the bank, moving the organizational chart around, and deleting certain personnel from the organization, this situation analysis process permits the Board of Directors and the senior management to understand more clearly the overall strengths and weaknesses of the organization. Please keep in mind that it is the ultimate responsibility of the Board of Directors to determine what changes must be made in order to improve the operations of the bank. On more than one occasion, certain key members of senior management have been determined through the situation analysis to be the major weaknesses of the institution. Thus, there is a two-edge sword to the situation analysis, since it does unearth incompetent and/or weak individuals, and thus becomes a threat to some members of management. We recommend that the Board of Directors be aware of the risks and rewards of the situation analysis, and to keep the overall challenges of the strategic planning process in mind when such a situation analysis is approved for the commercial bank.

Recommended Situation Analysis Report Format

Figure 12-2 is a recommended analysis report format. You, as the banker, know your bank best and you may wish to make variations, but this isat least at least a recommended format for your situation analysis report to be submitted to your Board of Directors.

Summary

The situation analysis is not a panacea. However, it does provide the Board of Directors and the senior management with an objective appraisal of the strengths and weaknesses of the commercial bank, and thus permits more efficient strategic planning. We have used the situation analysis as a means of gaining a better understanding of specific commercial banks and we recommend it highly to management and the Board of Directors for purposes of self analysis. In the long run the situation analysis can save a lot of time and money by pinpointing strengths and weaknesses immediately to guide changes made to improve the overall operation of the bank.

Bibliography

We have attempted to provide you with a selected current bibliography on strategic planning, especially those publications that are directly related to the commercial banking industry. This bibliography has been selected from all articles and publications which have appeared since 1980, with several selected works prior to 1980, but with emphasis on those articles which have been written so the lay commercial banker can easily understand them. They have also been chosen because of their empirical orientation, so that the reader can benefit from the articles in a realistic fashion at his or her own commercial bank.

Aaker, D.A. "How to Select a Business Strategy." *California Management Review* 26 (1984): 167–75.
Andrews, K.R. "Director's Responsibility for Corporate Strategy." *Harvard Business Review* 58 (1980): 30+.
Austin, D.V. and T.J. Scampini. "A Guide to Short-Term Strategic Planning." *The Bankers Magazine* 166 (1983): 62–8.
———. "Long-Term Strategic Planning." *The Bankers Magazine* 167 (1984): 61–6.

Bettinger, C. "Strategic Planning for the Commercial Lender." *Journal of Commercial Bank Lending* 66 (1983): 25–35.

Brown, J.E. "Survival Planning." *Mid-Continent Banker* 79 (1983): 52–4.

Buckenmyer, J.A. "Planning—I Haven't Got Time!" *Supervision* 44 (1982): 7–8.

Burke, R.G. and W.H. Dougherty. "Bank Strategies for the Balance of the 1980s." *The Magazine of Bank Administration* 59 (1983): 22–5.

Cohen, W.A. and S.C. Kennedy. "Strategic Planning Trends: The Whos, Whys, and Hows." *Direct Marketing* 47 (1984): 24+.

Collier, D. "How to Implement Strategic Plans." *Journal of Business Strategy* 4 (1984): 92–6.

Compton, E.N. "Bank Planning: A Status Report." *The Bankers Magazine* 164 (1981): 71–5.

"Consumer Goods Marketing and Banking Strategies." *Bankers Monthly* 100 (1983): 16+.

Cravens, D.W. "Developing Market Driven Strategies for Financial Institutions." *The Bankers Magazine* 167 (1984): 32–8.

Degueldre, J. "Corporate Planning and Modeling in a Large Bank." *Long Range Planning* 13 (1980): 43–50.

Dezember, R.S. "Customers are Shaping Bank Strategy." *The Magazine of Bank Administration* 59 (1983): 22–7.

Diecotiis, A.R. and J.J. DeMarco. "Does Financial Planning Suit Your Bank?" *ABA Banking Journal* 76 (1984): 43–5.

Dince, R.R. and W.R. Boulton. "BMA School Emphasizes Strategic Planning." *Bank Marketing* 15 (1983): 15–6.

Dissmeyer, V.M. "Five Operations Issues for the 80's." *ABA Banking Journal* 22 (1980): 89–91+.

Duhaime, I.M. and H. Thomas. "Financial Analysis and Strategic Management." *Journal of Economics and Business* 35 (1983): 413–440.

Ebeling, H.W. Jr. and T.L. Doorley. "A Strategic Approach to Acquisition." *Journal of Business Strategy* 3 (1983): 44–54.

Fannin, W.R. and C.B. Gilmore. "Managing with Deregulation: Management's New Challenge." *Managerial Planning* 33 (1984): 28–31.

Foster, M.J. and D.N. Foster. "Assessing the Effectiveness of Strategic Planning." *Omega: International Journal of Management Science* 10 (1982): 19–23.

Fronterhouse, G.W. and E.R. McPherson. "How Planning Is Used to Manage a BHC's Assets, Liabilities." *ABA Banking Journal* 73 (1981): 82–4.

Furash, E.E. "Here's the Newest Marketing Challenge: Targeting Profitability Through Strategic Pricing." *ABA Banking Journal* 75 (1983): 55.

Galbraith, C. and D. Schendel. "An Empirical Analysis of Strategy Types." *Strategic Management Journal* 4 (1983): 153–73.

Giroux, G.A. and P.S. Rose. "Financial Forecasting and Planning: Vital Tools for Bank Management." *The Canadian Banker and ICB Review* 87 (1980): 45–9.

Giroux, G.A. and S.H. Kratchman. "How Banks Forecast." *Management Accounting* 61 (1980): 39–44.

Hart, N.B. "Strategic Planning: Responsibility of the CEO." *The Magazine of Bank Administration* 60 (1984): 74–8.

Haugh, J.W. "Strategic Issues for the '80s." *Magazine of Bank Administration* 59 (1983): 14+.

———. "Strategic Planning and the Tax Function: Some Help." *The Magazine of Bank Administration* 57 (1981): 14+.

Havrilesky, T.M. and J.T. Boorman. *Current Perspectives in Banking: Operations, Management and Regulation*, 2nd ed. Arlington Heights, IL: AHM Publishing Corporation, 1980.

Holmberg, S.R. "Do CEOs Pay Lip Service Only to Strategic Planning?" *ABA Banking Journal* 72 (1980): 80+.

Holmberg, S.R. and H.K. Baker. "CEO's Role in Strategic Planning." *Journal of Bank Research* 12 (1982): 218–27.

Horovitz, J. "New Perspectives on Strategic Management." *Journal of Business Strategy* 4 (1984): 19–33.

Hosmer, L.T. "The Importance of Strategic Leadership." *Journal of Business Strategy* 3 (1982): 47–57.

Howland, W.G. "Corporate Planning—Prescription for Survival." *United States Banker* 95 (1984): 119–20+.

Jacquette, F.L. "Bank Balance Sheet Planning for the 1980's." *The Bankers Magazine* 163 (1980): 37–40.

Karkut, C.T. "The Growth Importance of Fee Income in Strategic Planning." *The Magazine of Bank Administration* 59 (1983): 20+.

Kellner, I.L. "Outlook 1984." *Bankers Monthly* 100 (1983): 4.

King, W.R. "Evaluating Strategic Planning Systems." *Strategic Management Journal* 4 (1983): 263–77.

King, W.R. "Implementing Strategic Plans Through Strategic Program Evaluation." *Omega: International Journal of Management Science* 8 (1980): 173–81.

Klaisle, W.J. "Fresh View of the Bank." *Bankers Monthly* 100 (1983): 13+.

Klein, H.E. *Growth, Profit and Long Range Planning in Banks.* Ann Arbor, MI: UMI Research Press, 1977.

————. "How Well Does Your Bank Plan for the Future?" *Managerial Planning* 30 (1982): 17–20.

————. "Impact of Planning on Growth and Profit." *Journal of Bank Research* 12 (1981): 105–9.

Kohn, S.J. and S.E. Rau. "Practical Approaches to Strategy Development." *The Bankers Magazine* 167 (1984): 56–64.

Krane, R.A. "Let's Plan our Future, Not Stumble into it." *ABA Banking Journal* 75 (1983): 43+.

Kudla, R.J. "The Current Practice of Bank Long-Range Planning." *Long Range Planning* 15 (1982): 132–8.

Leone, R.A. and J.R. Meyer. "Capacity Strategies for the 1980's." *Harvard Business Review* 58 (1980): 133–40.

Loughridge, R.F. "How to Assure Failure in Strategic Planning: Ten Sure-Fire Rules." *Managerial Planning* 30 (1982): 26.

Ludeman, D.H. "Banking in the '90s—A View from the '80s." *Journal of Commercial Bank Lending* 63 (1981): 4–11.

MacAvoy, R.E. "Strategic Planning." *Financial Executive* 48 (1980): 36–40.

McGillicuddy, J.F. "Bank Strategies for the 1980's." *Bankers Monthly* 97 (1980): 18+.

McLain, L.F., Jr. "How Strategic Planning Can Help Put Budgeting in Perspective." *Government Finance* 10 (1981): 35–40.

McRorie, J.S. "Strategic Planning: It Can Work at Your Bank." *Savings Bank Journal* 63 (1982): 17–9.

Mahmood, S.T. and M.M. Moon. "Competitive Analysis from a Strategic Planning Perspective." *Managerial Planning* 33 (1984): 37–42+.

Malernee, J.K. and G. Jaffe. "Integrative Approach to Strategic and Financial Planning." *Managerial Planning* 30 (1982): 35–43.

Mason, J.B. and M.L. Mayer. "Bank Management and Strategic Planning for the 1980's." *Long Range Planning* 12 (1979): 35–41.

Metzger, R.O., I.I. Mitroff and S.E. Rau. "Challenging the Strategic Assumptions of the Banking Industry." *The Bankers Magazine* 167 (1984): 29–34.

Metzger, R.O. and S.E. Rau. "Strategic Planning for Future Bank Growth." *Bankers Magazine* 165 (1982): 57–65.

Moger, H. "Planning for a Positive Future." *Mortgage Banker* 41 (1981): 78–82.

Morse, S. "The Power in Planning." *Management Today* (1984): 54–7.

Nadler, P.S. "What Strategies in a Changing Game?" *Bankers Monthly* 97 (1980): 9–12.

Naylor, T.H. "The Strategy Matrix." *Managerial Planning* 31 (1983): 4–9.

Oldfield, K. "Research and Planning Conference." *Bank Marketing* 15 (1983): 41–2.

O'Neill, H.M. *Turnaround Strategies in the Commercial Banking Industry.* Ann Arbor, MI: UMI Research Press, 1981.

Paine, F.T. and C.R. Anderson. *Strategic Management.* Chicago: The Dryden Press, 1983.

Prasad, S.B. "The Paradox of Planning in Banks." *Bankers Magazine* 167 (1984): 77–81.

Radford, K.L. *Strategic Planning: An Analytical Approach.* Reston, VA: Reston Publishing Company, Inc., 1980.

Robinson, R.B. and J. Pearce. "The Impact of Formalized Strategic Planning on Financial Performance in Small Organizations." *Strategic Management Journal* 4 (1983): 197–207.

Rose, P.S. "Bank Planning: Lessons from Experience." *The Canadian Banker and ICB Review* 89 (1982): 34–60+.

————. "Planning Elements, Steps and Strategies." *The Canadian Banker and ICB Review* 89 (1982): 50–5.

Rosenberg, J.L. "Long-Term Planning: Bank Districts Plan for the Future." *Federal Home Loan Bank Board Journal* 12 (1979): 8–15; 13 (1980): 11–17.

Sapp, R.W. "Banks Look Ahead." *Magazine of Bank Administration* 56 (1980): 33–40.

Shah, K. and P.J. LaPlaca. "Assessing Risks in Strategic Planning." *Industrial Marketing Management* 10 (1981): 77–91.

Stevenson, H. "What Lies Ahead." *The Ohio Community Banker* 6 (1983): 10+.

"Strategic Planning by Skilled Managers is Key to Survival from Deregulation." *Mid-Continent Banker* 79 (1983): 62–3.

Swinyard, W.B. "Strategy Development with Importance/Performance Analysis." *Journal of Bank Research* 10 (1984): 228–234.

Thompson, T.W. *Banking Tomorrow: Managing Markets Through Planning.* New York: Van Nostrand Reinhold Co., 1978.

Tull, C.L. "New Look at Bank Planning." *Managerial Planning* 28 (1980): 37–9.

Van Kirk, J.E. and K. Noonam. "Key Factors in Strategic Planning." *Journal of Small Business Management* 20 (1982): 1–7.

Williams, C.S. "A 'What If' . . . Plan." *The Ohio Community Banker* 5 (1983): 16+.

"Why Strategic Planning Doesn't Always Work." *Management Review* 72 (1983): 55–6.

Yalif, A. "Process of Strategic Planning in Banking." *Managerial Planning* 30 (1982): 19–24.

Index